D1418284

HOUSING IN THE 20TH AND 21ST CENTURIES   WOHNEN IM 20. UND 21. JAHRHUNDERT

Wolfgang Förster

Housing
in the 20th and 21st Centuries

Wohnen
im 20. und 21. Jahrhundert

PRESTEL München · Berlin · London · New York

CONTENTS

INHALT

THE ARCHITECTURE OF HOUSING

The car left the road across the dam and dropped its speed of sixty miles an hour to run gently through the residential quarters. The 'set-backs' permit vast architectural perspectives. There are gardens, games and sports grounds. And sky everywhere, as far as the eye can see. The square silhouettes of the terraced roofs stand clear against the sky, bordered with the lush green of the hanging gardens. The uniformity of the units that compose the picture throw into relief the firm lines on which the far-flung masses are constructed. Their outlines softened by the distance, the skyscrapers raise immense geometrical façades of glass, and in them is reflected the blue glory of the sky. An overwhelming sensation. Immense but radiant prisms.

Le Corbusier, *The City of Tomorrow and Its Planning*, 1929[1]

The first form of architecture was for residential building. Initially, people built homes for themselves, then for their gods — even if cultural historians generally tell us otherwise because temples are generally all that survive. The 4,700 year-old stepped pyramids at Saqqara in Egypt, the necropolis of the Old Kingdom, are the oldest existant examples of monumental architecture, imitating the structure of simple houses of stone, reed, wood and brick. As they were constructed of solid material, they record the design of the first buildings that humans erected for protection in an environment often hostile to life.

The earliest housing was still provisional and to some extent mobile, the residential structures of a nomadic or semi-nomadic society. Once the first cities were built, the construction of housing as buildings began, their basic characteristics changing later only in inessential features — in urban compactness, as standardised or regulated by law. In fact, the two forms of housing that were the subject of sharp ideological and urban planning controversy in the twentieth century already appeared in the cities of antiquity — dense and low (as in the famous hanging houses of Ephesus in Asia Minor, the atrium houses of the Roman upper classes, or the courtyard houses of the Chinese) or high-rise (as in the Roman port of Ostia or the proletarian districts of Rome). Even mixed types, such as are typical of modern, large cities, are found in the cultures of antiquity. The temporary housing that a hostel or inn constitutes and the functionally mixed type of the residentialcum-commercial block were commonplace in the rich trading metropolises along the transcontinental

Hanging house, Ephesus, **Turkey**
Hanghaus, Ephesos, Türkei

Das Auto hat den Damm und seine 100 Kilometer in der Stunde verlassen; sanft rollt es in ein Wohnviertel ein. Die Zahnschnittblocks erstrecken weithin die architektonischen Perspektiven. Gärten, Spiel- und Sportplätze. Alles beherrscht der Himmel, weit und frei. Die Wagrechte der flachen Dächer schneidet saubere Flächen heraus, von Grün übersponnen, das von den hängenden Gärten herrührt. Die Regelmäßigkeit der Elemente im einzelnen betont die feste Planung der großen, ausgedehnten Massen. Schon in dem Blau der Ferne sich lösend, erheben die Wolkenkratzer ihre großen geometrischen, ganz aus Glas gebildeten Flächen. In dem Glase, das ihre Fassaden von oben bis unten bekleidet, leuchtet der Azur und funkelt der Himmel. Ein einziger Glanz! Riesige, aber strahlende Prismen. Le Corbusier, *Städtebau*, 1929[1]

Die erste Architektur war Wohnungsbau. Zuerst errichteten die Menschen ihre eigenen Behausungen, dann jene ihrer Götter – auch wenn dies von der Kulturgeschichte meist anders überliefert wird, weil die Tempel als einzige Bauwerke überdauerten. Die 4700 Jahre alten Stufenpyramiden im ägyptischen Sakkara, der Nekropole des Alten Reichs, sind die älteste erhaltene Monumentalarchitektur und imitieren die Bauweise der einfachen Wohnhäuser aus Stein, Schilf, Holz und Ziegel. Da aus solidem Material erbaut, überliefern sie die Konstruktion jener ersten Bauten, die die Menschen als schützendes Dach in einer oft lebensfeindlichen Umwelt errichteten.

Die frühesten Wohnstätten waren noch temporär und teilweise mobil, die Wohnformen einer nomadischen oder halbnomadischen Gesellschaft. Mit der Entstehung der ersten Städte entwickelte sich auch der eigentliche Wohnungsbau, dessen Grundzüge sich später nur noch unwesentlich veränderten – urban verdichtet, standardisiert und durch Gesetze geregelt. Tatsächlich traten in den Städten der Antike schon jene zwei Grundformen des Wohnens in Erscheinung, die im 19. und 20. Jahrhundert Gegenstand heftiger ideologischer und städtebaulicher Kontroversen wurden: verdichteter Flachbau, etwa in den berühmten Hanghäusern von Ephesos in der heutigen Türkei, den Atriumhäusern der römischen Oberschicht oder den chinesischen Hofhäusern, andererseits Hochbau, wie in der römischen Hafenstadt Ostia oder den Proletariervierteln Roms. Selbst Mischformen, wie sie für die moderne Großstadt typisch sind, finden sich in den antiken Hochkulturen. Die temporäre Wohnform des Hotels und das funktional durchmischte Wohn- und Geschäftshaus waren vor allem in den reichen Handelsmetropolen entlang der transkontinentalen Karawanenrouten zu finden, wie etwa in Palmyra, Syrien. In keiner antiken oder auch mittelalterlichen Stadt findet sich dagegen der Bautyp des freistehenden Einfamilienhauses, denn dafür war städtischer Boden zu wertvoll und die Notwendigkeit, Städte gegen Angriffe zu verteidigen, erzwang Kompaktheit und Dichte.

Charakteristisch für die Stadt war zudem von Beginn an ihre Zonierung, Jahrtausende vor Tony Garniers Cité industrielle und der Charta von Athen. Auch wenn die meisten Städte viel kleiner waren als jene des Industriezeitalters, war Wohnen direkt im Verwaltungsbezirk oder etwa am Hafen nicht üblich, weil es schlicht zu teuer war. Somit entwickelten sich reine Wohnviertel und im übrigen auch erste sozialräumliche Segmentierungen. Dem Wohnviertel mit seiner spezifischen privaten Architektur stand das Bild der Agora gegenüber, Schauplatz und »Körper«[2] der Entwicklung der Demokratie. Der öffentliche Raum wurde zum bestimmenden Merkmal der Stadt und die Beziehung der privaten zur öffentlichen Sphäre zur Herausforderung, der sich die Architektur von Wohnvierteln zu stellen hatte und hat. Rückzug ins Private und Teilhabe am öffentlichen Leben spiegeln unterschiedliche gesellschaftliche und politische Entwicklungen wider und lassen sich an der Architektur der Wohnungsbauten deutlich ablesen. Jüngere Beispiele dafür sind beispielsweise der fließende Übergang zwischen Privatheit und Öffentlichkeit im sozialen Wohnungsbau der 1920er-Jahre oder die offenen Metastrukturen der 1960er-Jahre einerseits und die Privatisierung des öffentlichen Raums im England der Thatcher-Ära (»There is no such thing as society«) in den 1980er-Jahren andererseits.

caravan routes such as Palmyra (Syria). However, in no antique or mediaeval town do you find the detached, single-family home type. Urban land was too valuable for that, and the necessity to defend cities demanded compactness and density.

Typical of cities from the first was zoning, millennia before Tony Garnier's cité industrielle or the Athens charter. Even though most cities were much smaller than those in the industrial age, living directly in the administrative district or for example the port was not normal simply because it was too expensive. Thus purely residential districts developed along with the first socio-geographical sectorisation. In contrast to the residential quarter with its specifically private architecture were the agora (or marketplace), the arena and 'body' of democratic development.[2] Public space became the definitive feature of cities, and the relationship between private and public spheres a challenge that the architecture of residential quarters still faces and has to solve. The withdrawal into privacy and participation in public life reflect different social and political developments and can be clearly distinguished in the architecture of residential buildings. More recent examples of this can be seen in the fluid transition between private and public in the social housing of the 1920s, or the open superstructures of the 1960s, on the one hand, and the privatisation of public space in England during the Thatcher years ('There is no such thing as society') of the 1980s.

Architecture without residential building?

If residential building constitutes the oldest and most important form of architecture, one ought to be able to discern a corresponding regard for it in architectural theory. However, even a brief glance at the specialist literature on offer indicates that this is not the case. Keying in *housing* or *residential buildings* on internet search engines brings up hardly anything of much use, and a recent overview of contemporary architecture[3] documents eighty-six structures of all conceivable types – but not a single, multi-storey residential building. At the same time, there are an enormous number of publications on the market about other types of building such as museums, hotels, theatres, office blocks, transport and sports facilities. Was residential building really of such secondary importance in the twentieth century that current architectural theory can more or less ignore it completely?

It is instructive that even publications about housing deal almost exclusively with single-family homes, and generally expensive ones at that. Especially in the USA, this kind of residential building is contrasted with 'collective housing' – an expression that in architectural history hitherto referred only to a minor aspect of collective living, for example in the Soviet Union in the 1920s. Multi-storey residential buildings are thereby depreciated as not worthy of free individuals in a modern society and seen at best as a necessary evil in the less attractive parts of cities, or as temporary housing.

This attitude is carried over into the training of architects. At lectures in American universities, it causes astonishment if residential building – not to mention social housing – is discussed as a function of architecture in any way. The same applies to the connection between residential building and urban planning. This is a serious charge, bearing in mind that the greatest architects of the twentieth century were always dedicated urban planners as well. That applies to residential buildings of the Amsterdam School or the 'Neues Bauen' (New Building) in Germany as much as to the grand schemes of Le Corbusier, Auguste Perret or Oscar Niemeyer. Even where residential buildings never moved beyond utopias of urban design or (more often) were implemented only in fragmentary form, they were, nevertheless, among the great architectural achievements of the modern era.

Housing in an industrial age

Nineteenth-century housing faced two challenges and accordingly there were two parallel threads of debate – the social issue and the modern city. The mushrooming industrial towns and large-scale redesigns and expansions of cities such as Paris, Vienna and Berlin created the necessary parameters. Millions of people streamed into the urban agglomerations, if not always willingly. Whereas the state promoted the construction of an appropriate infrastructure and transport system – the latter corresponding to the conveyor belt of a Taylorian work organisation at urban planning level – residential housing was generally left to the private market.

The late Victorian and Edwardian eras (from the 1870s to 1914) were therefore periods of land speculation, standardised small homes behind Revivalist façades and housing shortages. Bad housing conditions

Architektur ohne Wohnungsbau?

Wenn Wohnungsbau die älteste und wichtigste Form der Architektur darstellt, so sollte man seine entsprechende Beachtung in der Architekturtheorie erwarten können. Es genügt jedoch ein kurzer Blick auf das aktuelle Angebot an Fachliteratur, um festzustellen, dass dies nicht der Fall ist. Stichworte wie ›Wohnungsbau‹ beziehungsweise ›housing‹ liefern zudem kaum brauchbare Ergebnisse bei der Recherche im Internet, und ein Übersichtswerk zur zeitgenössischen Architektur[3] dokumentiert unter 86 Bauwerken aller erdenklichen Sparten kein einziges mehrgeschossiges Wohnhaus. Gleichzeitig ist eine enorme Anzahl von Publikationen zu anderen Bauaufgaben wie Museen, Hotels, Theater, Verwaltungsgebäude, Verkehrsbauwerke, Sportanlagen auf dem Markt. War Wohnungsbau im 20. Jahrhundert wirklich so nebensächlich, dass ihn die aktuelle Architekturtheorie beinahe gänzlich vergessen kann?

Aufschlussreich ist, dass selbst jene Publikationen, die sich nach eigenem Verständnis mit dem Thema Wohnen befassen, fast ausschließlich das – meist aufwändige – Einfamilienhaus präsentieren. Dieser Wohnform wird heute vor allem in den USA das ›collective housing‹ gegenübergestellt – ein Ausdruck, der bislang in der Architekturgeschichte nur den kleinen Bereich des Kollektivwohnhauses, etwa in der Sowjetunion der 1920er-Jahre meinte. Mehrgeschossiger Wohnungsbau wird damit als einer modernen Gesellschaft freier Individuen nicht würdig abgewertet und allenfalls als notwendiges Übel in den weniger attraktiven Großstadtbezirken oder als temporäre Wohnform akzeptiert.

Diese Einstellung wird auch bei der Ausbildung von Architekten weitergetragen. Bei Vorlesungen an amerikanischen Universitäten erregt es schon Erstaunen, wenn Wohnungsbau – und erst recht Sozialwohnungsbau! – überhaupt als Aufgabe der Architektur thematisiert wird; ähnliches gilt für den Zusammenhang zwischen Wohnungs- und Städtebau. Ein schwerwiegender Vorwurf, waren doch die größten Architekten des 20. Jahrhunderts immer auch engagierte Städtebauer. Dies gilt für den Wohnungsbau der Amsterdamer Schule oder des deutschen Neuen Bauens ebenso wie für die Planungen Le Corbusiers, Auguste Perrets oder Oscar Niemeyers. Selbst dort, wo Wohnungsbauten im Rahmen städtebaulicher Entwürfe Utopie blieben oder, häufiger, nur fragmentarisch realisiert wurden, gehören sie zu den großen architektonischen Leistungen der Neuzeit.

Wohnen im Industriezeitalter

Den Wohnungsbau des 19. Jahrhunderts prägten zwei neue Herausforderungen und entsprechend parallel ablaufende Diskurse: die soziale Frage und die moderne Großstadt. Die neu entstandenen Industriestädte, aber auch die großzügigen Umgestaltungen und Erweiterungen bestehender Städte wie Paris, Wien und Berlin hatten dafür die Voraussetzungen geschaffen. Millionen Menschen strebten, nicht immer ganz freiwillig, in die urbanen Agglomerationen. Während der Staat den Bau von Infrastruktur und Massenverkehrsmitteln vorantrieb – letztere entsprachen auf städtebaulicher Ebene dem Fließband der tayloristischen Arbeitsorganisation –, blieb der Wohnungsbau meist dem privaten Markt überlassen. Die Gründerzeit von den 1870er-Jahren bis 1914 war daher von Grundstücksspekulation, standardisiertem Kleinwohnungsbau hinter historisierenden Fassaden und Wohnungsnot gekennzeichnet. Die schlechten Wohnverhältnisse führten immer wieder zu verheerenden Epidemien – einer der Gründe für die Wohnungsreformdiskussion des 19. Jahrhunderts.

Es gab zwei Möglichkeiten, dem Elend der Industriestadt zu begegnen: den Bau von städtischen Wohnhäusern als ›Arbeiterkasernen‹ oder die Planung von Gartenstädten. Beide Konzepte gingen auf Sozialutopien zurück – auf die palastartigen Phalanstères des Frühsozialisten Charles Fourier, die ansatzweise in der Familistère im französischen Guise (1880) realisiert wurden, beziehungsweise auf Robert Owens Gemeinschaftssiedlung New Harmony in Indiana, USA (1825). Ebenezer Howards Werk *Garden Cities of To-Morrow* führte 1899 zur Gründung der englischen Gartenstadtgesellschaft, einer Keimzelle des modernen Städtebaues, und zum Bau der ersten Gartenstadt Letchworth in Hertfordshire in England im Jahr 1903. Zwar waren schon früher Arbeitersiedlungen wie Saltaire bei Bradford (1853, seit 2001 Weltkulturerbe) und Port Sunlight bei Liverpool (1887) errichtet worden, doch standen dahinter

Ebenezer Howard, scheme for a garden city, 1899
Ebenezer Howard, Schema der Gartenstadt, 1899

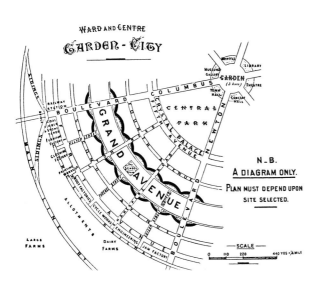

led time and again to devastating epidemics, which was one of the reasons for the debate about housing reform in the nineteenth century.

There were two possibilities for countering the misery of industrial cities: building urban housing as 'workers' barracks' or planning garden cities. Both concepts were derived from social utopias – the palatial *phalanstères* of the early socialist Charles Fourier, a prototype of which was the 'Familistère' in Guise in France (1880) – and Robert Owen's 'New Harmony' home colony in Indiana (1825). Ebenezer Howard's *Garden Cities of Tomorrow* led to the founding of the Garden Cities Association in 1899, a nucleus of modern urban planning, and the construction of Letchworth, the first garden city, in Hertfordshire, England, in 1903. There had of course been earlier worker estates such as Saltaire near Bradford (1853, a World Heritage site since 2001) and Port Sunlight near Liverpool (1887), but these were promoted by enlightened paternalist entrepreneurs. In contrast, Letchworth represented an autarkic small town for around 35,000 people. Barry Parker and Raymond Unwin's plan for it, with its irregular road network, blocks of terraced houses with service passages, business institutions and public buildings, became the prototype of garden cities generally. Moreover, the urban planning and social reform concepts were rigorously enforced. Details for standard enclosures and landscaping were specified, the keeping of domestic pets monitored and factory sirens and church bells forbidden. Garden cities were thus intended to become the perfect antithesis of noisy, dirty industrial towns. Of course, the reform principle was soon reduced to a planning exercise and the second, large scheme, Welwyn Garden City (1919), soon became a satellite town to London, with a large proportion of the population commuting to the metropolis. Nonetheless, what remained was still a major step forward in residential and environmental quality.

The often acrimonious controversy between low and high-rise development models was a continuing feature of architectural debate in the early twentieth century. Yet the two models had one thing in common – unlike the ideal cities of the Renaissance or the Absolutist schemes of the Baroque, their starting point was always the home, working from the micro-unit to the macro-entity, the smallest object to the town. Though the new divinities – industry, railways, banks, etc. – were allocated the accommodation they needed, the first actual consideration of all urban planning was the home function and its integration in a modern capitalist city.

And on to the unlimited city

Few architects in the late nineteenth century worked as intensively towards a symbiosis of urban planning and individual structures as Otto Wagner in Vienna – and few were able to realise ideas of this kind on such a scale. Wagner was aiming at no less than the 'unlimited city',[4] and assumed a regular doubling of the population of cities every thirty-to-fifty years. This growth would be accommodated within concentric circles, with radial boulevards clearly derived from Haussmann. Districts containing 100,000–150,000 inhabitants would each have a town centre, parks, etc. Wagner went further than the usual town planning ideology in that he, like Hendrik P. Berlage and Tony Garnier, developed specific financing models for urban expansion, assuming at least a temporary availability of building land for the city. Along with forward-looking transport structures, Wagner was able to construct several multi-storey residential buildings in Vienna where he himself was the client and which he often occupied. Among these are the splendid Art Nouveau buildings on the Wienzeile (1899) and more especially the buildings in Neustiftgasse and Döblergasse (1910), which were far ahead of their time. Behind standardised, fairly plain stucco façades lay anonymous apartments for the prosperous middle classes. The luxury was the amount of space on offer,

Otto Wagner, apartment house Neustiftgasse, Vienna, 1910
Otto Wagner, Mietshaus Neustiftgasse, Wien, 1910

aufgeklärte paternalistische Unternehmer. Letchworth verkörperte dagegen das Modell der von Landwirtschaft umgebenen autarken Kleinstadt für etwa 35 000 Einwohner. Der Plan für diese Gartenstadt von Barry Parker und Raymond Unwin mit seinem unregelmäßigen Straßennetz, Blocks aus Reihenhäusern mit innenliegenden Wirtschaftswegen, Betriebseinrichtungen und öffentlichen Gebäuden wurde zum Prototyp der Gartenstadt schlechthin. Das städtebauliche und gesellschaftliche Reformkonzept wurde zudem rigoros umgesetzt. So waren etwa einheitliche Einfriedung und Bepflanzung vorgeschrieben, das Halten von Haustieren wurde kontrolliert, Fabriksirenen und Kirchenglocken waren verboten. Die Gartenstadt sollte damit zum perfekten Gegenbild der lauten, schmutzigen Industriestadt werden. Freilich reduzierte sich ihr reformerischer Ansatz bald auf die Bebauungsform, und schon die zweite große Gartenstadt, Welwyn bei London (1919), wurde zum bloßen Vorort, dessen Bewohner zur Arbeit in die Großstadt pendelten. Was blieb, war immerhin der gewaltige Sprung in der Wohnungs- und Wohnumfeldqualität.

Die oft heftige Auseinandersetzung zwischen Anhängern des Flachbaus und des Hochbaus sollte die gesamte Architekturdebatte des frühen 20. Jahrhunderts prägen. Dennoch war eines beiden Konzepten gemeinsam: Sie gingen, im Gegensatz etwa zu den Idealstädten der Renaissance oder den absolutistischen Planungen des Barock, wieder ganz klar vom Wohnhaus aus, vom Kleinen zum Übergeordneten, vom Einzelobjekt zur Stadt. Zwar wurden auch den neuen Göttern – Industrie, Eisenbahn, Banken – die ihnen zustehenden Häuser errichtet, doch war der eigentliche Ausgangspunkt jeder städtebaulichen Planung die Funktion des Wohnens und seine Einbindung in die moderne kapitalistische Großstadt.

Auf dem Weg zur unbegrenzten Großstadt

Wenige Architekten des ausgehenden 19. Jahrhunderts strebten eine so intensive Symbiose zwischen Städtebau und Einzelobjekt an wie Otto Wagner in Wien – und wenige konnten derartig viel davon realisieren. Wagner wollte nicht weniger als die »unbegrenzte Großstadt«[4] und ging von einer regelmäßigen Verdoppelung der Einwohnerzahl moderner Großstädte innerhalb von 30 bis 50 Jahren aus. Dieses Wachstum sollte in konzentrischen Kreisen mit deutlich an Haussmann orientierten Radialboulevards erfolgen, wobei Bezirke mit jeweils 100 000 bis 150 000 Einwohnern über eigene Zentren und Grünanlagen verfügen sollten. Wagner ging jedoch über die eigentliche Stadtplanung hinaus, wenn er, wie später Hendrik P. Berlage und Tony Garnier, konkrete Finanzierungsmodelle für den Stadtausbau entwickelte und von einer zumindest temporären Verfügbarkeit des Baulandes durch die Stadt ausging. Neben zukunftsweisenden Verkehrsbauten konnte Wagner in Wien vor allem mehrere Wohnhäuser errichten, für die er meist selbst als Bauherr auftrat und die er oft auch selbst bewohnte. Dazu gehörten die prächtigen Jugendstilhäuser an der Wienzeile (1899), vor allem jedoch die Wohnhäuser Neustiftgasse und Döblergasse (1910), die ihrer Zeit weit voraus waren. Hinter gleichförmigen, nur wenig strukturierten Putzfassaden verbargen sich hier anonyme großbürgerliche Wohnungen; Luxus entfaltet sich im Raumangebot, während für Details wie Beleuchtung, Handläufe und Beschläge wie in den gleichzeitig entstandenen öffentlichen Gebäuden konsequent Industrieprodukte eingesetzt wurden. Wagner nahm damit Standardisierung und Vorfertigung im Wohnungsbau vorweg. Ohnehin ziehe es die Mehrzahl der Großstadtbewohner vor, »in der Menge als ›Nummer‹ zu verschwinden«.[5]

Hendrik P. Berlage, plan for Amsterdam South, 1902–17
Hendrik P. Berlage, Plan für Amsterdam-Süd, 1902–1917

Eine ähnlich konsequente Vorstellung von großstädtischem Wohnen, wenngleich mit einem weitreichenderen wohnungspolitischen Reformkonzept verbunden, entwickelte Hendrik P. Berlage in den Niederlanden, vor allem im Plan für Amsterdam-Süd (1902–1917). Stärker noch als bei Otto Wagner stellte hier der Wohnungsbau das Rückgrat der Stadtentwicklung dar. Ein 100 bis 200 Meter langer und 50 Meter breiter Baublock mit viergeschossiger Randbebauung und grünem Innenhof – eine Größenordnung, die sich aus der durchschnittlichen

while industrial products were systematically used for details such as lighting, banisters and fittings, as in the public buildings of the same period. Wagner was thereby a forerunner of standardisation and prefabrication in residential construction. In any case, most city-dwellers preferred to 'disappear in the crowd as a "number".'[5]

A similar logical notion of city living, albeit linked with a far-reaching housing policy reform concept, was developed by Hendrik P. Berlage in Holland, especially in the plan for Amsterdam South (1902–17). More even than with Wagner, residential buildings constituted the spine of urban development. A footprint 100–200 metres long and fifty metres wide, with a quadrangle of four-storey buildings around a green interior courtyard – the dimensions grew out of the average number of apartments of the housing co-operative building – it became a standard but never dogmatic grid. Berlage was able to exploit extraordinarily progressive Dutch housing legislation, including the Housing Construction Act of 1901 with its forward-looking framework planning. Moreover, his idea of a 'milieu unit' continues the tradition of Dutch canal-side houses with homogeneous but not uniform façades. In both cases, the planning task is to achieve homogeneity through variety, a 'homogeneous backdrop for the stylistic harmony'[6] of a dynamic, increasingly individualistic society. Berlage makes reference to Camillo Sitte,[7] whose rejection of showpiece neo-classical urban planning he shared.[8]

Building on Berlage's concept, younger architects such as Michel de Klerk planned housing estates that would leave their mark on housing construction in Europe in the 1920s. The basis for this was the founding of non-profit housing associations which made Holland a pioneer of modern social housing policy. For the first time, mass housing would become a symbol of cultural progress – working-class estates especially should manifest high artistic qualities. De Klerk became a protagonist of the Expressionist brick architecture of the Amsterdam School. In his best works such as the Spaarndammerplantsoen (1915) and Zaanstraat (1917–20) estates, collective form is combined with individualistic design. Though the Amsterdam School was criticised by representatives of Neue Sachlichkeit, including the De Stijl group, for its 'chaotic façade architecture' and 'romantic individualism',[9] the architects of Functionalism took over a number of basic principles from them, notably the carefully planned transitions from the private to the public sphere and the social ambition that 'nothing is too good for the worker, who has had to live so long without beauty' (De Klerk).[10]

At the other end of the urban planning spectrum but wholly comparable in terms of social reform was the thriving garden city movement, as both a consequence and antithesis of the (in many senses) dirty, industrial town. The first experiments in England were soon followed by numerous schemes on mainland Europe, including Hellerau in Dresden (Heinrich Tessenow, Hermann Muthesius, 1909), the Mathildenhöhe artists' colony in Darmstadt (Josef Maria Olbrich and others, 1908), Chemin de Fer du Nord in France (1919), Floréal and Le Logis near Brussels (1921), Monte Sacro in Rome (1920) and also the first American garden city at Radburn in New Jersey (1928). The estates of the Viennese *Siedlerbewegung*[11] constituted a special case. They arose in the immediate post-war years from the spontaneous occupation of land by tens of thousands of homeless people who, through the agency of newly founded co-operatives, constructed huge estates of terraced housing with the collaboration of prominent architects such as Adolf Loos and Josef Frank. It was not the individual small home but the social collective that was the visible face of this. All buildings had to be built in an organised way by the potential occupants, but only on completion of the whole estate were lots drawn for them. At the heart of the estates were model co-operative buildings with numerous communal installations. Incidentally, a fascinating detail is that the young architect Margarete Schütte-Lihotzky designed what is thought to be the first built-in kitchen in the world for a small worker's house in Vienna, long before she created her famous Frankfurt kitchen.

Victor Horta, Tassel House, Brussels, 1893–95
Victor Horta, Haus Tassel, Brüssel, 1893–1895

Michel de Klerk, Spaarndammerplantsoen, Amsterdam, 1915

Wohnungsanzahl der ausführenden Baugenossenschaften ergab – wurde zur Grundlage eines einheitlichen, jedoch niemals dogmatischen Rasters. Berlage konnte dabei auf die außerordentlich progressive holländische Gesetzgebung zurückgreifen, darunter das Wohnungsbaugesetz von 1901 mit seiner zukunftsweisenden Rahmenplanung. Zudem setzte seine Idee der »Milieueinheit« mit einheitlichen, aber nicht einförmigen Fassaden die Tradition der holländischen Grachtenhäuser fort. Beide Planungsvorgaben zielten auf Einheitlichkeit durch Vielfalt, auf »eine einheitliche Kulisse für die stilistische Harmonie«[6] einer zunehmend individualistischen Gesellschaft. Berlage berief sich dabei auch auf Camillo Sitte[7], dessen Ablehnung der repräsentativen klassizistischen Stadtplanung er teilte.[8]

Auf Berlages Konzept aufbauend, planten jüngere Architekten wie Michel de Klerk jene Wohnungsanlagen, die in den 1920er-Jahren den Wohnungsbau in Europa entscheidend prägen sollten. Grundlage dafür war die Gründung gemeinnütziger Wohnungsgesellschaften, die Holland zum Vorreiter einer modernen sozialen Wohnungspolitik machten. Erstmals wurde Massenwohnungsbau zum Symbol des kulturellen Fortschritts; insbesondere Arbeitersiedlungen sollten hohe künstlerische Qualitäten aufweisen. De Klerk wurde zum Protagonisten der expressionistischen Backsteinarchitektur der Amsterdamer Schule. In seinen besten Werken wie den Anlagen Spaarndammerplantsoen (1915) und Zaanstraat (1917–1920) verbinden sich große kollektive Form und individualistisches Design. Zwar wurde die Amsterdamer Schule von Vertretern der Neuen Sachlichkeit, darunter der De Stijl-Gruppe, wegen ihrer »chaotischen Fassadenarchitektur« und ihres »romantischen« Individualismus[9] kritisiert, doch übernahmen auch die Architekten des Funktionalismus wesentliche ihrer Grundprinzipien, vor allem die sorgfältig geplanten Übergänge von Privatsphäre und Öffentlichkeit und ihren sozialen Anspruch: »Nichts ist schön genug für den Arbeiter, der so lange ohne Schönheit leben musste« (de Klerk).[10]

Am anderen Ende des städtebaulichen Spektrums, aber sozialreformerisch durchaus vergleichbar, steht weiterhin die Gartenstadtbewegung – als Folge und zugleich Antithese der in mehrfachem Sinn schmutzigen Industriestadt. Den ersten Experimenten in England folgten bald zahlreiche Realisierungen auf dem europäischen Kontinent, darunter Dresden-Hellerau (Heinrich Tessenow, Hermann Muthesius, 1909), die Künstlerkolonie Mathildenhöhe in Darmstadt (Josef Maria Olbrich und andere, 1908), die Siedlungen der französischen Eisenbahngesellschaft Chemin de fer du Nord (1919), Floréal und Le Logis bei Brüssel (1921), Monte Sacro in Rom (1920), aber auch die erste amerikanische Gartenstadt, Radburn in New Jersey (1928). Einen Sonderfall stellen die Anlagen der Wiener Siedlerbewegung[11] dar. Sie entstanden in den ersten Nachkriegsjahren aus spontanen Landbesetzungen durch Zehntausende Wohnungslose, die mittels neu gegründeter Genossenschaften große Reihenhaussiedlungen unter Mitwirkung prominenter Architekten wie Adolf Loos und Josef Frank errichteten. Nicht das einzelne Kleinhaus, sondern das gesellschaftliche Kollektiv stand dabei im Vordergrund. So mussten alle Häuser in organisierter Selbstarbeit erbaut werden, wurden aber erst nach Fertigstellung der ganzen Siedlung verlost. Den Mittelpunkt der Anlagen bildeten repräsentative Genossenschaftshäuser mit zahlreichen Gemeinschaftseinrichtungen. Die Architektin Margarete Schütte-Lihotzky entwarf übrigens für ein einfaches Siedlerhaus in Wien die vermutlich erste Einbauküche der Welt, lange vor ihrer berühmten Frankfurter Küche.

Aufbruch in die Moderne

Überall befassten sich am Beginn des 20. Jahrhunderts prominente Architekten mit dem Wohnungsbau unter den Bedingungen der modernen Großstadt. So entwarf Hector Guimard, der heute in der Fachliteratur fast ausschließlich auf seine berühmten Metroeingänge und Art-Nouveau-Dekor reduziert wird, zwischen 1895 und 1910 mehrere durch ihre antiklassische Haltung und meisterhaften Materialeinsatz beeindruckende Wohnhäuser im Anteuil-Viertel des bürgerlichen 16. Pariser Arrondissements. In Brüssel war es Victor Horta, der den Jugendstil mit dem traditionellen belgischen Stadthaus verband und wie im Haus Tassel (1893) zu völlig neuen technischen und ästhetischen Lösungen fand.

The arrival of Modernism

At the beginning of the twentieth century, leading architects everywhere zeroed in on housing for modern city conditions. For example, between 1895 and 1910 Hector Guimard, who these days is reduced in literature almost exclusively to his famous Metro entrances and Art Nouveau stylings, designed several impressive housing blocks in the middle-class Anteuil district of Paris' 16th arrondissement. They were notable for their anti-classical manner and masterly use of materials. In Brussels it was Victor Horta who combined Art Nouveau with traditional Belgian town houses and came up with completely new technical and æsthetic solutions such as the Tassel house (1893).

Antoní Gaudí also pursued a consciously metropolitan style in his residential blocks in Barcelona, especially in the Casa Mila (La Pedrera, 1906–10). As with Wagner and Berlage, the existing urban scale was adopted, but behind the sculpturally designed façade there was a revolutionary design concept limiting the load-bearing parts to the external walls plus pillars and girders. Thus, long before the 'liberated living'[12] of New Building, the free allocation of internal space became possible. In the Casa Batlló built some years earlier, likewise located in the elegant Passeig de Gracia, Gaudí used sliding doors and windows that underlined the impression of a flowing space.

Around the same time, Adolf Loos created the showpiece residential-cum-commercial building on Michaelerplatz in Vienna (1909), an icon of early twentieth-century architecture, which was so radical it caused a major scandal. Instead of the classic vertical triple division, the façades clearly reflect the various functions of the building. Later, Loos also designed simple housing estates for workers and took up the cause of standardisation, while including functional garden layouts at the same time. His 'house with one wall' idea for cheap-to-build terraced buildings was partly implemented in the Heuburg estate. Loos's designs for stepped buildings in the social housing sector, on the other hand, were not pursued.

Above all it was two French architects, Auguste Perret and Henri Sauvage, who would leave an enduring legacy in city housing. In Perret's middle-class block in Paris' rue Franklin (1903) in the 16th arrondissement, the façade featured reinforced concrete for the first time in a residential building. Following the structuralism of Viollet-le-Duc,[13] the statics were reduced to the load-bearing frame, allowing the space within to be freely arranged, while pillars and girders were given prominence by means of lavish tiling. At the same time, however, Perret also stuck to a traditional façade composition, which would remain typical of his later work, especially in his reconstruction of Le Havre after World War II.

Henri Sauvage performed pioneering work in terracing. His first designs for stepped housing were submitted in 1909. Towards the end of the 1920s, they had developed into giant pyramids, as with, for example, the competition for the Porte Maillot development in Paris. It was no accident that one of these designs bore the name of Fritz Lang's utopian film *Metropolis*. Sauvage was particularly interested in health considera-

Auguste Perret, 25 rue Franklin, Paris, 1902   Antoni Gaudí, Casa Milá, Barcelona, 1906–10

Adolf Loos, Goldman & Salatsch Building, Vienna, 1909
Adolf Loos, Wohn- und Geschäftshaus Goldman & Salatsch,
Wien, 1909

Bewusst großstädtische Architektur verfolgte auch Antoni Gaudí bei seinen Wohnungsbauten in Barcelona, vor allem bei der Casa Mila (›La Pedrera‹, 1906–1910). Wie bei Wagner und Berlage wird der vorhandene städtische Maßstab aufgenommen, doch verbirgt sich hinter der plastisch ausgeformten Fassade ein revolutionäres Entwurfskonzept, das die tragenden Teile auf die Außenmauern sowie auf Stützen und Träger beschränkt. Eine freie Raumaufteilung wird damit lange vor dem »befreiten Wohnen«[12] des Neuen Bauens möglich. In der einige Jahre zuvor entstandenen Casa Battló, ebenfalls am eleganten Passeig de Gracia gelegen, setzte Gaudí zudem Schiebetüren und -fenster ein, die den Eindruck eines fließenden Raumkontinuums unterstreichen.

Etwa zur gleichen Zeit schuf Adolf Loos mit dem repräsentativen Wohn- und Geschäftshaus am Michaelerplatz in Wien (1909) eine Ikone der Architektur des frühen 20. Jahrhunderts, deren Radikalität zu einem ungeheuren Skandal führte. Anstelle einer klassischen vertikalen Dreiteilung spiegeln die Fassaden die verschiedenen Funktionen des Hauses klar wider. Loos entwarf später auch einfache Arbeitersiedlungshäuser und setzte sich intensiv mit Standardisierung, aber auch mit Gartenbau auseinander. Sein ›Haus mit einer Mauer‹, ein billig zu errichtendes Reihenhaus, wurde in der Siedlung Heuberg teilweise realisiert. Loos' Entwürfe für Terrassenhäuser im sozialen Wohnungsbau wurden dagegen nicht weiter verfolgt.

Vor allem aber waren es zwei französische Architekten, die den großstädtischen Wohnungsbau nachhaltig prägen sollten: Auguste Perret und Henri Sauvage. Bei Perrets großbürgerlichem Wohnhaus an der Rue Franklin (1903) im 16. Pariser Arrondissement bestimmte erstmals im Wohnungsbau die sichtbare Eisenbetonkonstruktion das äußere Erscheinungsbild. Dem Strukturalismus von Viollet-le-Duc[13] folgend, reduziert sich die Statik auf das tragende Skelett und ermöglicht eine freie Raumaufteilung; Stützen und Träger werden durch die aufwändigen Keramikverkleidungen der Ausfachungen stärker hervorgehoben. Gleichzeitig hielt Perret jedoch an einer traditionellen Fassadenkomposition fest, die auch für sein späteres Werk – vor allem beim Wiederaufbau von Le Havre nach dem Zweiten Weltkrieg – charakteristisch bleiben sollte.

Henri Sauvage wurde zum Pionier des Terrassenhauses. Schon 1909 legte er erste Entwürfe für abgestufte Wohnungsbauten vor, die sich gegen Ende der 1920er-Jahre etwa im Wettbewerbsentwurf für die Bebauung an der Porte Maillot in Paris zu gigantischen Pyramiden entwickelten. Nicht zufällig trug einer dieser Entwürfe den Namen von Fritz Langs utopischem Film *Metropolis*. Sauvage ging dabei von hygienischen Überlegungen aus. Im Kampf gegen die Tuberkulose sollten die ausreichend belichteten und belüfteten Terrassenwohnungen eine Art großes »städtisches Sanatorium«[14] darstellen. Dem grundlegenden Problem jedes Terrassenbaus, der Nutzung des unbelichteten Innenraums, wollte er mit Großgaragen und anderen städtischen Einrichtungen begegnen. Das erste realisierte Projekt in Paris in der Rue Vavin (1912) nahm sich bescheiden aus. 1922 erhielt Sauvage jedoch die Möglichkeit, 78 Sozialwohnungen in einem achtgeschossigen, terrassierten Bau an der Rue des Amiraux zu errichten – mit seinen weißen Keramikfassaden und dem innenliegenden Schwimmbad bis heute ein technisch und sozial außergewöhnlich beeindruckendes Beispiel großstädtischen Wohnungsbaus.

Interessanterweise fanden sich gerade diese abgetreppten Baukörper auch in den zeitgenössischen Architekturutopien, die einen radikalen Bruch mit der Stadt des 19. Jahrhunderts propagierten, so etwa bei Paul Scheerbart (»Diese Terrassenformation der Etagen wird natürlich die langweilige Frontarchitektur der Backsteinhäuser rasch verdrängen«[15]) und bei Antonio Sant'Elia. Die futuristische Stadt müsse »einer großen, lärmenden Werft gleichen und in allen ihren Teilen flink, beweglich, dynamisch sein; das futuristische Haus muss wie eine riesige Maschine sein. Der Aufzug soll sich nicht mehr wie ein Bandwurm im Schacht des Treppenhauses verbergen; die überflüssig gewordenen Treppen müssen verschwinden, und die Aufzüge sollen sich wie Schlangen aus Eisen und Glas emporwinden.«[16]

Soziale Stadt und Internationaler Stil

Die meisten dieser städtebaulichen oder sozialrevolutionären Konzepte konnten erst unter den völlig veränderten gesellschaftlichen Bedingungen der 1920er-Jahre baulich umgesetzt werden. Die politischen Umwälzungen

Henri Sauvage, rue des Amiraux, Paris, 1922   Antonio Sant'Elia, La Città nuova, 1914

tions. The plentifully lit and airy stepped-back apartments would become a kind of 'urban sanatorium'[14] in the fight against tuberculosis. To solve the basic problem of such buildings, namely how to use the unlit interior space, he proposed installing large garaging and other urban facilities. The first project actually completed, in rue Vavin in Paris (1912), was rather modest but, in 1922, Sauvage was given an opportunity to construct seventy-eight social housing units in an eight-storey, stepped apartment block in rue des Amiraux. To this day, it remains technically and socially an extraordinarily impressive example of a metropolitan residential block, with its white-tiled façades and inside swimming pool.

Interestingly, these stepped structures in particular also occur in contemporary descriptions of architectural utopias propagating a radical break with the nineteenth-century city, for example by novelist Paul Scheerbart ("These stepped formations of the storeys will of course soon oust the boring façade architecture of brick houses")[15] or Antonio Sant'Elia. The Futurist city had to be "like a large, noisy shipyard and be snappy, mobile and dynamic, while the Futurist residential building would have to be like a huge machine. The lift should not hide itself in the shaft of the stairwell like a tapeworm. The stairs would be superfluous and lifts should rise like snakes of iron and glass."[16]

The social city and international style

Most urban planning or social revolutionary concepts were actually only implemented in bricks and mortar under the completely different social conditions of the 1920s. In most West European cities, the political changes following World War I had brought social democratic administrations to power and installed committed urban planners in influential positions. Among these more powerful communes were cities such as Rotterdam, Frankfurt and Berlin. In Rotterdam, J. J. P. Oud (a co-founder of the De Stijl group) gave Functionalism that vital helping hand with his Hoek van Holland and De Kiefhoek housing estates; Frankfurt, under city councillor Ernst May, became a centre of standardised housing construction, as well as Berlin under construction director Martin Wagner. Two European cities were in a special position: Lyons, where Tony Garnier had an opportunity – at least in part – to implement his pioneering designs for a cité industrielle, and 'Red Vienna' with its (architecturally) moderately Modernist but (socio-politically) highly radical, communal housing programme. Within a very short time, tens of thousands of small homes grouped around courtyards or in super-blocks had been constructed in Vienna, which were supplemented by ample communal institutions such as baths, laundries, kindergartens, libraries and healthcare institutions. The architects involved included figures such as Adolf Loos, Josef Hoffmann, Clemens Holzmeister and Peter Behrens. The

nach dem Ersten Weltkrieg hatten in den meisten westeuropäischen Großstädten sozialdemokratische Regierungen an die Macht und engagierte Städteplaner in die entscheidenden Positionen gebracht. Zu diesen erstarkten Kommunen gehörten Städte wie Rotterdam, wo J. J. P. Oud, Mitbegründer der De Stijl-Gruppe, mit den Wohnungsanlagen Hoek van Holland und De Kiefhoek dem Funktionalismus zum Durchbruch verhalf; Frankfurt am Main, das unter dem Stadtrat Ernst May ein Zentrum des standardisierten Wohnungsbaus war sowie Berlin unter dem Baudirektor Martin Wagner. Zwei europäische Städte nahmen eine Sonderstellung ein: Lyon, wo Tony Garnier die Gelegenheit erhielt, seine bahnbrechenden Entwürfe für eine Cité industrielle zumindest teilweise zu verwirklichen, und das ›Rote Wien‹ mit dem architektonisch gemäßigt modernen, sozialpolitisch aber radikalsten Kommunalwohnungsprogramm. Innerhalb kürzester Zeit errichtete die Stadt Zehntausende Kleinwohnungen in Höfen und Superblocks, die durch großzügige Gemeinschaftseinrichtungen wie Bäder, Waschküchen, Kindergärten, Bibliotheken und Gesundheitsinstitutionen ergänzt wurden. Unter den Architekten fanden sich beispielsweise Adolf Loos, Josef Hoffmann, Clemens Holzmeister und Peter Behrens. Der revolutionäre Kollektivwohnungsbau der jungen Sowjetunion fiel dagegen bald der Bürokratie zum Opfer, beeinflusste aber später Architekten wie Le Corbusier.

An den Rändern Europas verlief die Entwicklung gemäßigter, doch gab es herausragende Einzelpersönlichkeiten. In Dänemark realisierte Arne Jacobsen seinen »pittoresken«[17] skandinavischen Funktionalismus; in Schweden baute Sven Markelius, später Stadtplaner von Stockholm, sein bekanntes Kollektivwohnhaus in der Ericssongatan; und in Norditalien verband Giuseppe Terragni in genialer Weise den strengen Rationalismus seiner Zeitgenossen mit lokalen urbanen Strukturen. Das Neue Bauen, vertreten durch das 1919 von Walter Gropius gegründete Bauhaus, die verschiedenen Werkbundausstellungen in Stuttgart, Wien, Zürich, Breslau/Wroclav, Prag und Stockholm sowie durch die CIAM (Congrès Internationaux d'Architecture Moderne), wurde rasch zum Internationalen Stil. Architekten wie Ludwig Mies van der Rohe und Le Corbusier entwickelten in den 1930er-Jahren jene architektonischen Prinzipien, die nach dem Zweiten Weltkrieg weltweit zum Durchbruch gelangen sollten. Bemerkenswert sind auch die Bauten von Maxwell Fry in London, jene von Brinkmann & van der Vlugt mit Willem van Tijen in den Niederlanden sowie zahlreiche Wohnungsbauten in Tel Aviv, das in den 1930er-Jahren zu einem Zentrum der modernen Architektur wurde. Andere Bauten sind weniger bekannt, vielleicht weil sie abseits des architektonischen Mainstream geplant wurden, wie etwa die außergewöhnliche Art-Déco-Anlage Gratte-Ciel von Môrice Leroux in Lyon oder zahlreiche Gebäude in der neu entstehenden rumänischen Metropole Bukarest.

Karl Ehn, Karl-Marx-Hof, Vienna, 1927–30
Karl Ehn, Karl-Marx-Hof, Wien, 1927–1930

J.J.P. Oud, Spangen, Rotterdam, 1919–20

Die Suche nach einer neuen Urbanität

Nach 1945 war der Wohnungsbau in Europa zunächst durch Wiederaufbauprogramme geprägt. Viele von ihnen folgten dem Ideal der aufgelockerten Stadt mit Wohnungsanlagen geringer Dichte als Alternative zur ›ungesunden‹ Großstadt der Gründerzeit. Doch es gab auch bemerkenswerte Planungen, die auf eine neue Urbanität ab-

revolutionary collective housing of the young Soviet Union, on the other hand, soon fell victim to bureaucracy, but nevertheless influenced later architects such as Le Corbusier.

On the margins of Europe, development was more moderate, but there were nonetheless outstanding personalities. In Denmark, Arne Jacobsen set about realising his 'picturesque'[17] Scandinavian Functionalism; in Sweden, Sven Markelius – later, a Stockholm urban planner – constructed his well-known Ericssongatan collective housing and, in northern Italy, Giuseppe Terragni came up with a brilliant combination of the strict rationalism of his contemporaries and local urban structures. New Building, represented by Walter Gropius's Bauhaus founded in 1919, the various Werkbund exhibitions in Stuttgart, Vienna, Zurich, Breslau/Wroclaw, Prague and Stockholm plus CIAM (Congrès Internationaux d'Architecture Moderne), quickly became the international style. In the 1930s, architects such as Mies van der Rohe and Le Corbusier developed the architectural principles that would become generally accepted after World War II. Also notable were the buildings of Maxwell Fry in London, Brinkmann & Van der Vlugt with Willem van Tijen in Holland and numerous housing schemes in Tel Aviv, which in the 1930s was a centre of modern architecture. Other buildings are less known, perhaps because they were planned away from the architectural mainstream, for example the extraordinary Art Deco Gratte-Ciel estate of Môrice Leroux in Lyons or numerous buildings in the newly sprouting Rumanian metropolis of Bucharest.

The search for a new urbanity

Post-1945 housing construction in Europe was all about reconstruction. Many schemes followed the ideal of a more loosely arranged city with housing estates of lower density, as an alternative to the 'unhealthy' metropolis of the Victorian era. But there were also remarkable schemes that sought a new kind of urbanism – partly classical Modernist (Auguste Peret in Le Havre), partly popular neo-realist (Mario Ridolfi and Ludovico Quaroni in Tiburtino, Rome). Le Corbusier was also given the opportunity to build several of his large housing machines and, in New Towns in England and satellite urban developments in Scandinavia, housing became the most visible expression of the modern social state. However, the real centre of innovative work increasingly moved out of the European arena to North American cities such as Chicago and New York, Central and South American cities such as Havana, Rio de Janeiro and Brasilia, or Casablanca in North Africa. Nonetheless, the international style was still susceptible to noticeable regional variation.

Archigram, Plug-in City, 1964–66

In the mood of radical change in the 1960s and '70s, work on urban utopias continued throughout the world, furthered by architects such as Yona Friedman, Haus-Rucker-Co, Friedrich St Florian, Hans Hollein, Kisho Kurokawa, Paul Maymont, Archigram, Superstudio, Archizoom and others.[18] Metastructures and prefabricated elements were intended to make for greater flexibility and the democratic appropriation of space. Few of the projects were actually realised, one of the few – albeit reduced in size – being Moshe Safdie's famous Habitat '67 in Montreal, Canada (1967).

When in the 1980s cities came to be seen as 'inhospitable',[19] there was a change in paradigm from large-scale structures to architecture on a more human scale, combined with the renovation of the existing city. Examples of the former were the projects by Ralph Erskine in England and Scandinavia and Herman Hertzberger in Holland. The second development showed up most clearly within the scope of the International Building Exhibition (IBA) in Berlin in 1987, in which architects such as Aldo Rossi, Rob Krier, Oswald Mathias Ungers, Hans Hollein, Herman Hertzberger, Hans Kollhoff, Arata Isozaki and Vittorio Gregotti were involved. The shortage of city-centre building land led to spectacular brownfield projects such as the port of Amsterdam, London, Lower Manhattan/New York and Hamburg. Other buildings responded in the shape of higher densities, the multiple use of available land and industrial construction methods, high-rise building, long-term ecological construction methods and sophisticated implants in existing urban.

zielten – teils klassisch-modern wie Auguste Perret in Le Havre, teils neorealistisch-populär wie Mario Ridolfi und Ludovico Quaroni in Tiburtino, Rom. Le Corbusier konnte nun mehrere seiner großen Wohnmaschinen realisieren und in den englischen New Towns und den skandinavischen Trabantenstädten wurde der Wohnungsbau zum sichtbarsten Ausdruck des modernen Sozialstaats. Der Schwerpunkt des innovativen Schaffens verlagerte sich jedoch zunehmend auf außereuropäische Schauplätze, in nordamerikanische Städte wie Chicago und New York, in mittel- und südamerikanische Städte wie Havanna, Rio de Janeiro und Brasilia oder das nordafrikanische Casablanca. Der Internationale Stil erfuhr dabei deutlich regionale Ausprägungen.

In der Aufbruchstimmung der 1960er- und 70er-Jahre wurde weltweit an Städteutopien gearbeitet, durch Architekten wie Yona Friedman, Haus-Rucker-Co, Friedrich St. Florian, Hans Hollein, Kisho Kurokawa, Paul Maymont, Archigram, Superstudio, Archizoom und andere.[18] Metastrukturen und vorgefertigte Elemente sollten flexible Nutzungen und demokratische Raumaneignung ermöglichen. Nur wenige dieser Projekte wurden realisiert, darunter das berühmte Habitat '67 von Moshe Safdie in Montreal, Kanada (1967).

Unter dem Eindruck der »unwirtlichen« Städte[19] vollzog sich ab den 1980er-Jahren ein Paradigmenwechsel von der Großstruktur zu einer Architektur des menschlichen Maßstabs und zur Stadtreparatur. Ersteres wurde beispielsweise in den Projekten von Ralph Erskine in England und Skandinavien und von Herman Hertzberger in den Niederlanden sichtbar. Die zweite Entwicklung zeigte sich am eindrucksvollsten im Rahmen der Internationalen Bauausstellung (IBA) in Berlin 1987 unter Beteiligung von Architekten wie Aldo Rossi, Rob Krier, Oswald Mathias Ungers, Hans Hollein, Herman Hertzberger, Hans Kollhoff, Arata Isozaki und Vittorio Gregotti. Der Mangel an innerstädtischen Bauflächen führte außerdem zu spektakulären Umnutzungsprojekten wie beispielsweise im Amsterdamer Hafen, in London, in Lower Manhattan in New York oder in Hamburg. Andere Bauten reagierten durch höhere Dichte, Mehrfachnutzung von Freiflächen und industrielle Baumethoden, Hochhäuser, nachhaltige ökologische Bauweisen oder raffinierte Implantate in bestehende urbane Strukturen auf die vielfältigen neuen Herausforderungen des Wohnens am Ende des 20. Jahrhunderts.

Town villas in the Tiergarten district, International Building Exhibition (IBA) Berlin, 1980–85
Stadtvillen im Tiergartenviertel, Internationale Bauausstellung (IBA) Berlin, 1980–1985

Zugleich verändert sich, nicht zuletzt durch die ubiquitäre Verfügbarkeit der neuen Medien, die städtische Planungsebene. Stadt- und Wohnquartiere werden zunehmend dynamisch begriffen, und an die Stelle des ausschließlich territorial definierten Raums treten prozessuale Räume als Folien für immer unterschiedlichere gesellschaftliche Realitäten. Während sich so die Architektur im Wohnungsbau global vereinheitlicht und – zumal in den Werken der Stararchitekten – weltweit austauschbar wird, differenziert sie sich zunehmend nach sozialer Stellung, Bildung, Familienmodell und (Selbst-)Bild ihrer Nutzer, die ihr als Konsumenten mit kurzfristig wechselnden Ansprüchen gegenübertreten.

Megastädte

Der Jahrtausendwechsel ist auch von einer weitgehenden Desillusionierung in Bezug auf städtebauliche, architektonische und technische Experimente im Wohnungsbau gekennzeichnet – ein Ende der Utopien? Nicht unbedingt. Eindeutig feststellbar sind allenfalls widersprüchliche Entwicklungen: Einerseits zieht sich die Architektur auf ihre ursprüngliche Aufgabe, den Bau von Einzelobjekten, oft von Solitären ohne Bezug zu ihrer wenig attraktiven Umgebung, zurück; andererseits entstehen in einer neuerlich auftretenden antiurbanen Haltung Gated Communities, die eine zunehmende gesellschaftliche und sozialräumliche Polarisierung widerspiegeln.[20]

Am stärksten treten diese Disparitäten in den rasant wachsenden Megastädten in den Entwicklungsländern zutage. Erstmals lebt am Beginn des 21. Jahrhunderts die Hälfte der Weltbevölkerung in Städten, und die

At the same time, things changed at urban planning level, not least because of the general availability of the new media. Urban and residential districts were increasingly seen as dynamic entities, and processual spaces ousted exclusively territorially defined spaces as models for ever more diverse social realities. Whereas architecture in housing tended towards global uniformity and, particularly in the works of star architects, became interchangeable worldwide, there was an increasing degree of differentiation reflecting social status, education, family model and the (self-)image of their users, who now featured as consumers with changing short-term ambitions.

Megacities

The turn of the millennium was also marked by widespread disillusionment with urban planning, architectural and technical experiments in housing. Does this mean the end of utopias? Not necessarily. Certainly there is a degree of contradictory movement – on the one hand architecture veering towards its previous task of constructing single objects, often stand-alone buildings without any relation to their rather unattractive surrounding, on the other a recent trend towards anti-urban gated communities, reflecting an increasing social and topographical polarisation.[20]

These disparities are most pronounced in the rapidly growing megacities of the emergent world. At the beginning of the twenty-first century, for the first time ever, half the world's population lived in cities, the overwhelming proportion of them in slums. Housing construction can react in various ways to this: with flexible schemes, accepting basically limitless growth, by re-appropriating and re-coding public space, as in the Cité Manifeste in Mulhouse/France or numerous British estates, or most radically with projects where developed building land with services connected is made available, as for example in Indore in India, in a return to anonymous but orderly self-construction.

Housing – a continuum of architectural history?

This 'serviced land' approach does, astonishingly, reflect the layout of the oldest cities known to us. Disregarding the huge differences in sizes and technical possibilities, it is today, as it was thousands of years ago, a question of the same challenges and tasks – dividing up the land and its availability, the relationship between private and public, zoning with simultaneous functional and social intermixing, the treatment of natural resources, creating the technical and social infrastructure and achieving a desired or desirable density. Housing construction also contains a potential for conflict – in the relationship between standardisation and artistic freedom, the conflicting needs of privacy and publicness, mobility and roots and, ultimately, in the relationship between the individual and the social collective. Even the subject of the careful handling of local building traditions and the *genius loci* is not all as new as globalisation and technical progress would give one to suppose. Just consider the universality of housing construction in the Roman Empire or the cultural dominance of British, French and Dutch colonial architecture.

If one analyses the development of residential construction in the twentieth century, one thing is surprising more than anything else – the persistence of traditional forms of housing. Despite all the social ups-and-downs and architectural utopias, human homes have not changed radically in the last hundred years. Is the reason for this that homes – people's 'third skins' –not only reflect a physical need but a psychological one as well? An opportunity to withdraw into privacy and at the same time have a place of public presentation? A fulfilment of childhood desires, but also an expression of past traumas? The gods and their houses may change, but housing may be considered a continuum in the long history of architecture.

1 LeGates, Stout, 1996, p. 374 f.
2 Sennett, 1995, p. 66.
3 Jodidio, 2001
4 Wagner, 1911
5 Ibid., p. 21
6 Benevolo, 1978, vol. 1, p. 426
7 Sitte, 1889
8 Grinberg, 1982, p. 42
9 see e.g. Grinberg, 1982, p. 50, 52
10 Gemeentelijke Dienst Volkshuisvesting, 1986, p. 7

11 Novy/Förster, 1985
12 Giedion, 1929
13 Viollet-le-Duc, 1872
14 Dethier, Grillet, Guilheux, 1994, p. 198 f.
15 Conrads, 1964, p. 29
16 Ibid., p. 32
17 Benevolo, 1978, vol. 2, p. 275
18 e.g. Dethier, Grillet, Guilheux, 1994
19 Mitscherlich, 1965
20 e.g. Sassen, 1994

überwiegende Mehrzahl von ihnen in Slums. Wohnungsbau kann darauf unterschiedlich reagieren: mit flexiblen Konzepten im Rahmen eines grundsätzlich akzeptierten unbeschränkten Wachstums, mit der Wiederaneignung und Neukodierung des öffentlichen Raums (wie in der Cité Manifeste in Mulhouse, Frankreich oder zahlreichen britischen Siedlungsbauten) oder, am radikalsten, mit Projekten, bei denen erschlossenes Baugebiet (serviced land) zur Verfügung gestellt wird, wie beispielsweise im indischen Indore, einer Rückkehr zum anonymen, aber geordneten Selbstbau.

Kontinuum der Architekturgeschichte?

Tatsächlich ähnelt dieser ›serviced land‹-Ansatz in verblüffender Weise der Anlage der ältesten uns bekannten Städte. Sieht man von den natürlich gewaltigen Unterschieden der Dimensionen und der technischen Möglichkeiten ab, so handelt es sich heute ebenso wie vor Tausenden von Jahren um die gleichen Fragestellungen und Aufgaben: die Aufteilung des Bodens und die Verfügbarkeit über ihn, das Verhältnis von privaten zu öffentlichen Bereichen, Zonierung bei gleichzeitiger funktionaler und sozialer Durchmischung, den Umgang mit natürlichen Ressourcen, die Bereitstellung der technischen und sozialen Infrastruktur und die Erreichung einer gewünschten oder erforderlichen Dichte. Wohnungsbau behält auch sein Konfliktpotential: im Verhältnis von Standardisierung zu künstlerischer Freiheit, in den gegensätzlichen Bedürfnissen nach Privatheit und nach Öffentlichkeit, nach Mobilität und nach Verwurzelung, letztlich im Verhältnis des individuellen Menschen zum gesellschaftlichen Kollektiv. Selbst die Thematik des oft wenig schonenden Umgangs mit lokalen Bautraditionen und dem genius loci ist nicht so neu, wie es Globalisierung und technischer Fortschritt vermuten lassen – man betrachte nur die Universalität des Wohnungsbaus im Römischen Reich oder die kulturelle Dominanz der britischen, französischen und holländischen Kolonialarchitekturen.

Analysiert man die Entwicklung des Wohnungsbaus im 20. Jahrhundert, so verblüfft jedoch vor allem eines: die Beharrlichkeit tradierter Wohnformen. Sämtlichen gesellschaftlichen Umwälzungen und Architekturutopien zum Trotz haben sich die menschlichen Behausungen in den letzten hundert Jahren keineswegs radikal verändert. Liegt es daran, dass Wohnen, die ›dritte Haut‹ des Menschen, neben physischem immer auch psychisches Bedürfnis ist? Rückzugsmöglichkeit ins Private und zugleich Ort öffentlicher Selbstdarstellung? Erfüllung von Kindheitswünschen, aber auch Ausdruck erlittener Traumata? Die Götter und ihre Häuser mögen wechseln – Wohnungsbau kann dagegen als der ›rote Faden‹, das Kontinuum in der langen Geschichte der Architektur betrachtet werden.

1 Le Corbusier, *Städtebau*, Stuttgart, Faksimile-Wiedergabe der 1. Auflage 1929, 1979, S. 144
2 Sennett, 1995, S. 66
3 Jodidio, 2001
4 Wagner, 1911
5 Ebd., S. 21
6 Benevolo, 1978, Band 1, S. 426
7 Sitte, 1889
8 Grinberg, 1982, S. 42
9 Ebd., S. 50 und S. 52
10 Gemeentelijke Dienst Volkshuisvesting, 1986, S. 7
11 Novy/Förster, 1985
12 Giedion, 1929
13 Viollet-le-Duc, 1872
14 Dethier, Grillet, Guilheux, 1994, S. 198f.
15 zitiert nach: Conrads, 1964, S. 29
16 Ebd., S. 32
17 Benevolo, Band 2, 1978, S. 275
18 siehe zum Beispiel: Dethier, Grillet, Guilheux, 1994
19 Mitscherlich, 1965
20 siehe zum Beispiel: Sassen, 1994

HOUSING IN THE 20TH CENTURY

When, at the end of World War I, Old Europe had collapsed and given way to the emergence of completely new economic and administrative systems, the development of 'new housing for a new society' became a top issue of the political agenda. Moreover, the revolutionary spirit of post-war Europe forced municipal governments – now mostly dominated by Social-Democrats – to act quickly. Within a few years cities like Vienna, Frankfurt, Berlin, Hamburg, Lyons, Rotterdam and Amsterdam established pioneering social housing systems, involving the élite of contemporary architects.

At the same time, architects in the Soviet Union experimented with radical solutions for 'collective housing', and the late 1920s and early 1930s witnessed a number of model housing estates built by the national Werkbund organisations. The so-called International Style spread over all of Europe, notably Germany, France, and the Netherlands, reaching the more peripheral areas – Scandinavia, Italy, Romania, and even Israel – in somewhat moderate forms which also picked up on local building traditions.

The urban reconstruction programmes after WW II were influenced by opposing ideas: 'housing machines' and pre-fabrication on one hand, vernacular housing schemes (as in Le Havre or Rome) and New Towns (in England and Sweden) on the other hand. But the centre of modern housing development had moved to the Americas, with groundbreaking new architecture being realized in cities like Chicago, Rio and Brasilia.

While the 1960s and 1970s saw the development of utopian superstructures with pre-fabricated meta-systems, the growing pluralism in society gradually led to more diversification in housing. Architecture was understood as a social responsibility again and, at the end of the twentieth century, housing became an integral part of 'city repair' programmes, brown-field developments and sustainable urban planning efforts.

The following twenty-five chapters focus on housing schemes which may serve as prototypes for new developments: in terms of architecture and building techniques – built by well-known as well as by almost forgotten architects; in social terms – from 'housing for minimum existence' to luxurious apartment complexes; in terms of building typology – low-rise estates, solitary slabs, tower blocks, in-fills; and, last but not least, in terms of geographical location, with the focus slowly spreading from Europe to America and to the southern hemisphere. These prototypes are complemented by examples of housing schemes which, in spite of varying conditions, represent similar ideas and concepts.

Der Zusammenbruch des alten Europa und die revolutionäre Stimmung nach dem Ersten Weltkrieg zwangen die nun meist sozialdemokratisch regierten Großstädte, innerhalb kurzer Zeit völlig neue Sozialwohnungssysteme aufzubauen. Städte wie Wien, Frankfurt, Berlin, Hamburg, Lyon, Rotterdam und Amsterdam realisierten bahnbrechende Wohnungsbauten unter Mitwirkung der Architektenelite ihrer Zeit.

Gleichzeitig experimentierten Architekten in der Sowjetunion mit Kollektivwohnhäusern. Die 1920er- und 30er-Jahre waren von den verschiedenen Werkbund-Ausstellungen und von der Verbreitung des Internationalen Stils, ausgehend von Deutschland, Frankreich und den Niederlanden, geprägt. In peripheren Regionen wie Skandinavien, Italien, Rumänien oder Israel nahm dieser auch lokale Stilmerkmale auf.

Der Wiederaufbau nach dem Zweiten Weltkrieg war von gegensätzlichen Tendenzen gekennzeichnet: einerseits von ›Wohnmaschinen‹ und Vorfertigung, andererseits von lokal geprägter Architektur und New Towns. Doch verlagerte sich der Schwerpunkt des modernen Wohnungsbaus von Europa nach Nord- und Südamerika, in Städte wie Chicago, Rio de Janeiro oder Brasilia.

Den utopischen Superstrukturen und vorgefertigten Metasystemen der 1960er- und 70er-Jahre folgten ein zunehmender gesellschaftlicher Pluralismus und eine Diversifizierung des Wohnens. Architektur wurde wieder als gesellschaftliche Verantwortung verstanden. Am Ende des 20. Jahrhunderts wurde Wohnungsbau zum integralen Bestandteil von Stadtreparatur-Programmen, großflächigen Umnutzungen und nachhaltigen Planungsansätzen.

Die folgenden 25 Kapitel beschreiben Wohnungsbauten, die als Prototypen für neue Entwicklungen stehen – im Bereich von Architektur und Bautechnik, errichtet von weltbekannten, aber auch von fast vergessenen Architekten; im sozialen Sinn, von der Wohnung für das Existenzminimum bis zu luxuriösen Apartmentkomplexen; im Sinn der Bautypologie, als Flachbau, Scheibenbau, Hochhaus oder Baulückenschließung; und nicht zuletzt in geographischer Hinsicht, da sich der Schwerpunkt der Entwicklung schrittweise von Europa nach Amerika und auf die südliche Hemisphäre verlagert. Den beschriebenen Prototypen sind jeweils weitere Beispiele zugeordnet, die ähnliche Ideen und Konzepte verkörpern, wenngleich oft unter völlig anderen Rahmenbedingungen.

THE 1920S AND '30S:
NEW HOMES FOR A NEW SOCIETY

1920ER- UND 30ER-JAHRE:
NEUES WOHNEN FÜR EINE NEUE GESELLSCHAFT

THE TENANTS' PALACE   DER VOLKSWOHNUNGSPALAST

Hubert Gessner
Reumannhof
Vienna Wien   **Austria** Österreich   **1924–1926**

Among the efforts to overcome the cramped living conditions of pre-WW I private speculative housing the programme carried out by 'Red Vienna' – the world's first metropolis governed by Social-Democrats – was unrivalled in Europe. Between 1923, after introducing an ear-marked and strongly progressive housing tax, and 1934 the city built about 70,000 low-cost municipal flats for rent (*Gemeindewohnungen*) on some 400 estates. While apartment plans and sizes were subject to regulations stipulated by the city housing department – consisting mostly of the traditional kitchen/living room (*Wohnküche*), hall, w.c., and one or two bedrooms – the architectural concepts varied as the new projects were commissioned to a large number of private architects. Still, even today, these estates are easy to recognize. This is firstly due to the extensive use of standardized building elements – windows, entrance doors, sanitary equipment – and, secondly, to the evolution of a distinct urban typology which radically transformed the existing urban fabric. Breaking with the

traditional distinction of street, closed block, and inaccessible courtyard the new estates offered green courtyards and a comprehensive infrastructure for collective use by all city residents.

When in 1924 a large open area along Gürtel Street – Vienna's second ring road on the site of the former outer defence line – was being redeveloped the city commissioned the architect Hubert Gessner to build the Reumannhof Estate as the centre – piece of a social housing area with several thousand dwellings. This was no coincidence as Gessner, a student of Otto Wagner's and a socialist, had already planned a number of buildings for Social-Democratic organisations. Thus, as the 'party architect', he was to develop nothing less than the model housing for the society of the future. This included several distinctive features, such as the creation of a collective space mentioned above, the integration of a communal infrastructure – baths, laundries, kindergartens, health institutions, libraries, workers' clubs, and, probably most importantly, an entirely new access system. Stair-

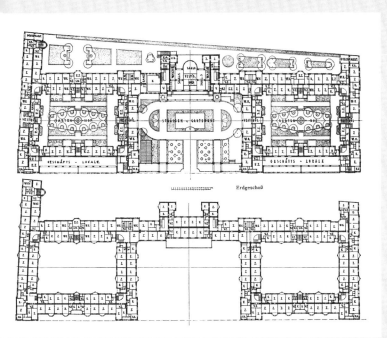

Erdgeschoß

cases were now approached from the courtyards. Thus he created a sequence from public via semi-public-to private spaces, a 'destabilization of traditional concepts of boundary'.[1]

Reumannhof became even more significant as Gürtel Street was soon conceived as the 'Ring Road of the Proletariate' – the counterpart of the 19th-century bourgeois Ringstrasse. Consequently, Gessner underlined the importance of the estate with a twelve-storey central building (Vienna's first 'skyscraper') flanked by two six-storey perimeter blocks. Although the tower had to be reduced to six storeys plus two levels with artists' ateliers, the 180-metre street front is impressive. Its baroque composition is 'filled with cultural memory and local associations',[2] reminiscent of 18th-century palaces. Modernist architects like Josef Frank,[3] although himself a distinct anti-functionalist, mocked it as a petit-bourgeois *Volkswohnungspalast* (literally a tenement palace for the people) but this term quickly gained a positive connotation, reflecting the high – and until today unbroken – popularity of the new estates. In fact, it seemed easier for a proletarian clientele to accept their vernacular classicism, as well as their formal pathos, than dogmatic, modernist, Neues Bauen architecture. At the same time, Vienna also denounced industrialized building methods as traditional construction provided more jobs. In any case, Gessner had set the model: reconfigurating the existing urban topography rather than destroying it. This was taken up by many other architects – among them Josef Frank, Adolf Loos, Margarete Schütte-Lihotzky, Peter Behrens, Josef Hoffmann, Clemens Holzmeister – and by wellknown 'superblocks' such as Rabenhof or Karl-Marx-Hof. Gradually these buildings shaped the city itself, surviving the destruction of 'Red Vienna' by fascism, in 1934, as 'built ideas'.[4]

1 Blau, 1999, p. 227
2 Blau, 1999, p. 257
3 see the critical remarks by the International Town Planning and Housing Congress, Vienna, 1926; also Schuster, 1926
4 Tafuri, 1995

Der Wohnungsbau des ›Roten Wien‹ – der ersten sozialdemokratisch regierten Millionenstadt der Welt – war europaweit einzigartig. Zwischen 1923 und 1934 wurden rund 70 000 Gemeindewohnungen in etwa 400 Anlagen gebaut. Obwohl von unterschiedlichsten Architekten errichtet – darunter Josef Frank, Adolf Loos, Margarete Schütte-Lihotzky, Peter Behrens, Josef Hoffmann, Clemens Holzmeister –, sind sie aufgrund der Standardisierung der Bauteile (Fenster, Haustore, Sanitäreinrichtung) sowie des völlig neuartigen Erschließungssystems bis heute klar erkennbar. Die Treppenhäuser werden nunmehr vom halböffentlichen Hof, zugleich Zugangs- und Kommunikationsraum, erschlossen. Die traditionelle Trennung von Straße, geschlossenem Block und unzugänglichem Innenhof wurde dadurch aufgehoben. Die Stadtstruktur sollte nicht zerstört, sondern radikal neu figuriert werden.

Hubert Gessner schuf am Gürtel, der ›Ringstraße des Proletariats‹, mit dem Reumannhof ein Beispiel für diesen neuen, mit zahlreichen Gemeinschaftseinrichtungen wie Bädern, Waschküchen, Kindergärten, Bibliotheken und Gesundheitsstützpunkten ausgestatteten Typus. Mittelhof, Arkaden und dominierender Mitteltrakt (ursprünglich als Hochhaus geplant) zitieren lokale Stilelemente. Von Architekten wie Josef Frank als kleinbürgerlicher »Volkswohnungspalast« kritisiert, schien ihr klassisches Vokabular für die Bewohner leichter rezipierbar als das dogmatische Neue Bauen. Bauten wie der Reumannhof, der Rabenhof oder der Karl-Marx-Hof überlebten daher als »gebaute Ideen« (Manfredo Tafuri) die Zerstörung des Roten Wien durch den Faschismus im Jahr 1934.

Fritz Schumacher   Jarrestadt   Hamburg   Germany Deutschland   1928–1932

The Viennese approach to low-cost housing – which could be described as moderately modern in its stylistic expression but groundbreaking in its societal and urbanistic concept – was, of course, studied carefully all over Europe. One of the cities which aimed at a similarly new role for public spaces in low-cost housing estates was Hamburg where Fritz Schumacher, a co-founder of the Deutscher Werkbund, had been nominated Building Director in 1909. He developed an innovative system of 'organic' urban growth based on large new social housing areas around the historic city centre.[5] One of these, Jarrestadt (1928–32), was subject to a competition, with finally ten architects participating in the housing projects. Following Schumacher's master plan, most of the four to six-storey buildings enclose large, semi-public courtyards. All flats are orientated to two sides and communal facilities have been integrated. The architecture features a local mix of Neues Bauen modernism and traditional brick façades. Details like corner solutions have been especially carefully designed. One of the most impressing buildings is the Friedrich-Ebert-Hof by the architect Friedrich Ostermeyer.

Per Olof Hallmann, Sven Wallander   Rödaberget   Sweden Schweden   1925   Höög & Morssing Architects   Birkastan, Stockholm   Sweden Schweden   1927–1928

In Scandinavian residential architecture functionalism was only
reluctantly adopted, and some of the best 1920s housing areas
remained in a moderate nordic classicism. This includes the
beautiful Stockholm housing area at Birkastan (Höög & Morssing
Architects, 1927–28), the Rödaberget working-class area (Per Olof
Hallmann, Sven Wallander, 1925),[6] and the Norrköping workers'
housing estate (Erik Lallerstedt, 1919–22)[7] with their carefully
designed vernacular elements.

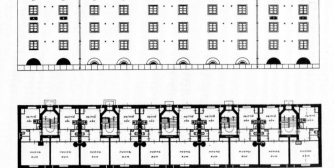

Gunnar Taucher Mäkelänkatu Helsinki Finland Finnland **1924–1926**

In Helsinki, Finland, the rather austere Mäkelänkatu apartment building by Gunnar Taucher (1924–26)[8] shows the direct influence of the early Viennese municipal housing estates.

5 C.f. e.g. Hipp, 1992
6 Lindvall, 1992, pp. 51, 52; also: Andersson, 1997, p. 109
7 Lindvall, 1992, p. 55
8 Norri, 1999, p. 174

Vergleichbare Bauten, wenn auch in kleinerem Maßstab, wurden unter anderem in Hamburg (Jarrestadt von Fritz Schumacher, 1928–1932), in Stockholm (Rödaberget von Per Olof Hallmann und Sven Wallander, 1925) und in Helsinki (Wohnanlage Mäkelänkatu von Gunnar Taucher, 1924–1926) realisiert.

Erik Lallerstedt Norrköping Sweden Schweden **1919–1922**

ARTS AND FUNCTIONALISM   KUNST UND FUNKTIONALISMUS

Jacobus Johannes Pieter Oud
Hoek van Holland Housing Complex   Wohnanlage Hoek van Holland
Hoek van Holland   The Netherlands Niederlande   1924–1927

J. J. P. Oud, who in his early years was strongly influenced by Hendrik P. Berlage and by his cooperation with the Munich architect Theodor Fischer, was appointed Municipal Housing Architect of Rotterdam in 1918. As one of the founders of the De Stijl movement and as a convinced socialist he strove to connect social-oriented urban planning with the ideas of functionalism. After a number of more traditional housing estates – Spangen (1918–20) and Tusschendijken (1920–21) – Oud designed the Hoek van Holland estate, radically breaking with the Dutch grid pattern of closed courtyards and with the prevailing architectural style of neo-plasticism. The estate consists of two identical, two-storey buildings, almost classical in their use of symmetry. The upper apartments have balconies to both sides, the lower ones have gardens facing a public park and small front gardens.

The whole development is characterized by a dynamic interplay of private and communal spaces; while the long block, with its continuous strip of balconies and its standardized win-

dows and doors, underlines the concept of collective urban living, low brick walls along the front gardens re-establish the perception of individual houses; similarly the transition between the public park and private gardens at the back is treated very carefully. Materials may be cheap but have a high stylistic quality: white plaster walls dominate – as in most functionalist buildings – but are accentuated by differently coloured, brick elements at strategic points; doors and fences were painted blue, pillars were red, and the blinds were striped red and white. These elements were cheap and easy to maintain, but it was also Mondrian's colour scheme applied to social housing. Understandably, Benevolo argues that Oud's housing estates belong 'to the most convincing works of so-called functionalism'[1] in its literal sense, as the technical accuracy of each element contributes to the intensity of the architectural expression.

1 Benevolo, vol. 2, 1978, p. 98

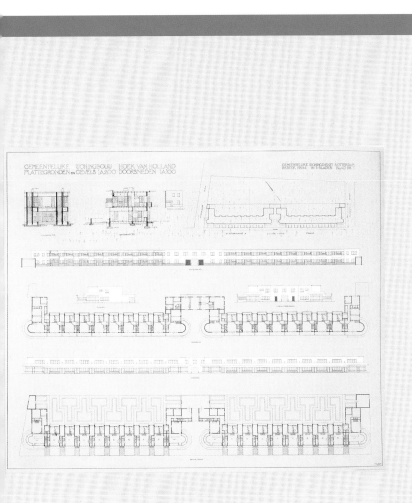

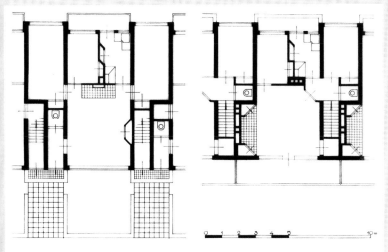

Jacobus Johannes Pieter Oud, Mitbegründer von De Stijl und überzeugter Sozialist, wurde 1918 Leiter der städtischen Wohnungsabteilung von Rotterdam. Nach eher traditionellen Planungen in den Wohnvierteln Spangen (1918–1920) und Tusschendijken (1920/21) stellte der Wohnbau in Hoek van Holland einen radikalen Bruch mit dem holländischen Blockrastersystem und seinen geschlossenen Innenhöfen, aber auch mit dem vorherrschenden Stil des Neoplastizismus dar. Die in ihrer Symmetrie beinahe klassische Anlage besteht aus zwei identischen zweigeschossigen Gebäuden, wobei die oberen Wohnungen beidseitig Balkone, die Wohnungen im Erdgeschoss Gärten und Vorgärten haben. Ein spannungsvolles Verhältnis zwischen privaten und öffentlichen Räumen charakterisiert den Bau. Während die über die gesamte Länge gezogenen Balkone und die standardisierten Fenster und Türen das kollektive Planungskonzept betonen, stehen die niedrigen Ziegelmauern der Vorgärten für das individuelle Einfamilienhaus. Ähnlich sorgfältig wird der Übergang zwischen öffentlichem Park und privaten Gärten behandelt. Die Materialien sind zwar kostengünstig, aber architektonisch wirkungsvoll eingesetzt. Wie in fast allen funktionalistischen Bauten dominieren weiß verputzte Wände, die aber durch verschiedenfarbige Ziegelelemente unterbrochen werden. Türen und Zäune waren blau, Pfeiler rot und die Sonnenblenden rot-weiß gestreift – Mondrians Farbspektrum übertragen auf den sozialen Wohnungsbau.

J.J.P. Oud   De Kiefhoek   Rotterdam   The Netherlands Niederlande   1925–1929

Oud further developed his functionalist planning approach in the nearby De Kiefhoek workers' settlement (1925–29), a classical garden city[2] in spite of its revolutionary architectural vocabulary. The small houses are absolutely identical, and the impression of unity is deliberately strengthened by the continuous strips of windows on both levels. Corner solutions are dealt with very sensitively, defining the transition from private to public spaces. As most gardens are not visible from the road, however, tenants were able to make alterations and extensions which create an utterly varied picture at the back. Thus, for Oud, functionalism was neither art for art's sake – probably one of the reasons for his increasing conflict with the De Stijl group – nor a simple matter of standardization, but rather a logical way to achieve the best quality housing. "I long for a home that satisfies all the requirements of my love of comfort, but for me a house is more than a 'machine à habiter'."[3]

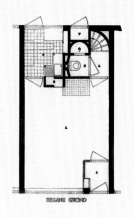
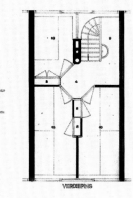

WONINGBOUW KIEFHOEK ROTTERDAM 1925

BEGANE GROND

VERDIEPING

Die nahe gelegene Wohnanlage **De Kiefhoek**, die Oud 1925 plante, stellt dagegen – trotz ihrer revolutionären funktionalistischen Architektur – eine klassische Gartenstadt dar. Die Einheit der völlig identischen Reihenhäuser wird durch Fensterbänder auf beiden Ebenen betont. Innovative Ecklösungen definieren den sensiblen Übergang von öffentlichen zu privaten Bereichen. An den Gartenseiten konnten die Mieter jedoch individuelle Veränderungen vornehmen. Für Oud war Funktionalismus weder ›l'art pour l'art‹ noch auf Fragen der Standardisierung beschränkt, sondern ein logischer Weg zu höchster Qualität im Wohnungsbau – vermutlich einer der Gründe für seinen zunehmenden Konflikt mit der De Stijl-Gruppe.

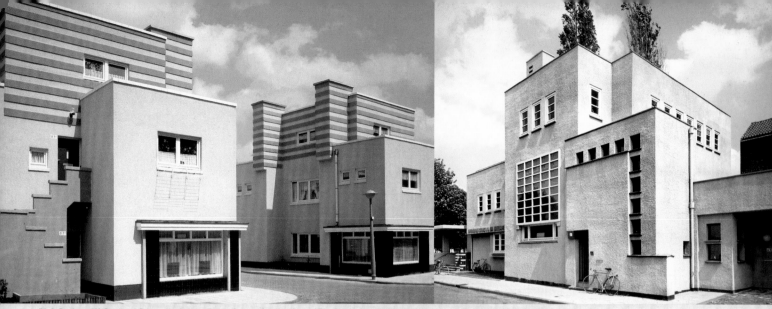

Dick Greiner, W. Greve, J.B. van Loghem   **Betondorp**   **Amsterdam**   **The Netherlands** Niederlande   **1923–1928**

In a country where the early tradition of social housing had not been interrupted by the war Oud was, of course, not the only architect striving for a new architectural expression in large-scale housing. Among the considerable number of residential areas built in the 1920s the so-called Betondorp (Concrete Village) at Amsterdam-Watergraafsmeer, by the architects Dick Greiner, W. Greve, and J.B. van Loghem is outstanding. Amsterdam's huge urban expansion programme of had made bricks rare and building in general more and more expensive; this led the architects to search for alternatives. At Watergraafsmeer they experimented with various building systems based on pre-fabricated, multi-layered, concrete elements[4] which were produced on the construction site. Maintenance would later be a problem[5] but the variety of the architecture in this 900-unit estate is still impressing. Linked stylistically more to the earlier Amsterdam school of expressionism than to International Style functionalism, it proves that several options existed for a further development of housing prototypes.

2   Grinberg, 1982, p. 98
3   J.J.P. Oud, in Von Technik und Innendekoration, vol. 36, Stuttgart 1925
4   Pennink, Bruyn, 1965
5   Gemeentelijke Dienst Volkshuisvesting, 1986, p.7

Ein weiteres Beispiel für den innovativen niederländischen Wohnungsbau der 1920er-Jahre ist das so genannte **Betondorp** von **Dick Greiner**, **W. Greve** und **J.B. van Loghem** in **Amsterdam**, dessen rund 900 Wohnungen als Folge der steigenden Ziegelpreise aus Betonfertigteilen errichtet wurden. Die eindrucksvolle Architektur steht dem Amsterdamer Expressionismus näher als dem Funktionalismus – ein Beweis dafür, dass es auf dem Weg zu künftigen Wohnformen mehrere Optionen gab.

THE SOCIAL CITY   DIE SOZIALE STADT

Ernst May
Römerstadt
Frankfurt/Main   Germany Deutschland   1927–1928

Frankfurt/Main became one of the centres of German modern housing when the architect Ernst May, who had previously worked with Raymund Unwin on the Hampstead Garden City project, was nominated Head of the City Planning Department in 1925. May proposed an innovative system of decentralized housing estates[1] which were to create some 15,000 affordable, yet up-to-date housing units within the following five years. The programme concentrated on industrial construction methods with pre-fabricated building parts, functionally optimized floor plans and low-density linear structures with extensive open areas and roof terraces. May expressed his opinion that "after food and clothing, housing is man's most important material need. Therefore is has to be produced in large quantities and in the best possible quality."[2] The Nidda Valley became the core of the huge urban development, taking in Römerstadt, Praunheim, Westhausen, Höhenblick, Raimundstraße and Miquelallee estates. The Römerstadt estate alone had more than 1,200 flats. Equally impressive is May's master plan for the large Heimatsiedlung estate in Sachsenhausen, and the Hellerhof estate by Mart Stam. Though highly standardized each of these estates has its own characteristics – using for example curved, linear, or zigzag blocks – as different architects were commissioned. While May himself clearly favoured terraced housing, most of the new estates were built as three or four-storey blocks due to financial restraints. As a form of compensation most flats were given balconies as well as small allotments for the tenants to grow their own vegetables. The famous garden architect Leberecht Migge designed special vegetation plans which had to be followed strictly.[3]

For the first time, housing was designed as an integral part of the general urban fabric. Housing areas were connected to the social infrastructure, traffic was separated from pedestrian ways and higher buildings were positioned to ease noise levels towards the main roads. The architecture followed the credo of Neues Bauen, with flat roofs and flat façades, supplemented by balconies and horizontal strip windows as structural elements. Later glass verandas were introduced. Not only the construction process was to be optimized, however, but the daily life of the tenants themselves. May invited the architect Margarete Schütte-Lihotzky – who had worked with Adolf Loos and had designed what was probably the world's first built-in kitchen for a simple workers' settlement in Vienna[4] – to develop a standardized kitchen for the Frankfurt housing estates. The famous 'Frankfurt kitchen'[5] represented a radical break with the traditional kitchen/living room (or *Wohnküche*) in workers' flats by introducing a thoroughly standardized laboratory-type kitchen unit of only six square metres with built-in furniture and with an astounding range of labour and space-saving innovations (dish drainers, foldaway ironing boards, waste dispensers). About 10,000 of these kitchens were installed in the new Frankfurt housing estates. When the economic crisis stopped the Frankfurt building programme in 1930 both May and Schütte-Lihotzky continued their work with standardized city planning in the Soviet Union.

1 Nerdinger, 2000, p. 50
2 Das Neue Frankfurt, 1930, p. 37
3 Ernst May-Gesellschaft, 2005
4 Novy/Förster, 1985, pp. 78, 79
5 C.f. Noever (ed.), 1993, pp. 88–99

Unter dem Stadtrat für Bauwesen und Städtebau Ernst May wurde Frankfurt am Main ab 1925 zu einem Zentrum des modernen Wohnungsbaus. May schlug dezentrale, durchgrünte Wohngebiete in industrialisierter Bauweise vor. Der Schwerpunkt der neuen Stadtentwicklung lag im Niddatal mit Siedlungen wie der mehr als 1200 Wohnungen umfassenden Römerstadt, Praunheim, Westhausen, Höhenblick, Raimundstraße und Miquelallee. Ebenso beeindruckend sind Mays Heimatsiedlung in Sachsenhausen und die Hellerhofsiedung von Mart Stam. Innerhalb von fünf Jahren wurden 15000 Wohnungen mit optimierten Grundrissen errichtet. Trotz Standardisierung unterscheiden sie sich in ihrer Architektur, da verschiedene Architekten beteiligt waren. May bevorzugte zwar Reihenhäuser, doch wurden aus Kostengründen hauptsächlich drei- bis viergeschossige Blocks realisiert. Fast alle Wohnungen verfügen über Balkone oder eigene Gärten, für die der berühmte Gartenarchitekt Leberecht Migge verbindliche Bepflanzungspläne entwarf.

Erstmals wurde Wohnungsbau als Teil der Stadtentwicklung mit kompletter Infrastruktur geplant. Auch die tägliche Lebensführung sollte erleichtert werden. Auf Einladung Mays entwarf die österreichische Architektin Margarete Schütte-Lihotzky, die zuvor für ein einfaches Siedlerhaus in Wien die vermutlich erste Einbauküche entwickelt hatte, eine standardisierte Küche. Die ›Frankfurter Küche‹, die in rund 10 000 Sozialwohnungen eingebaut wurde, ersetzte die traditionelle Wohnküche durch eine Arbeitsküche mit zahlreichen innovativen arbeits- und raumsparenden Details. Als die Wirtschaftskrise 1930 das Frankfurter Bauprogramm zum Erliegen brachte, setzten May und Schütte-Lihotzky ihre gemeinsame Tätigkeit in der Sowjetunion fort.

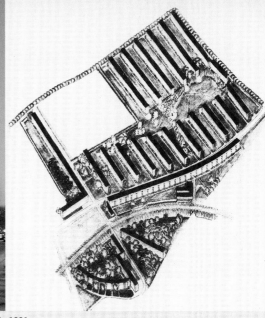

Fred Forbát, Walter Gropius, Hugo Häring, Hans Scharoun   Siemenstadt   Berlin   Germany Deutschland   1928–1931

The Frankfurt mass housing experiment was not the only one in Germany. Most of the major cities were then ruled by the Social-Democrats who introduced workers' housing schemes, with Berlin – under its dynamic Building Director Martin Wagner – playing a leading role. Wagner had initiated the foundation of a union-owned housing association to exclude profit-oriented building companies from public housing programmes. As early as 1924 he had also planned the first experimental housing estate in Berlin-Lichtenberg using the 'panel' construction principle. His master-piece, however, was to become the plan for the huge Siemensstadt urban development which was executed by several architects from 1928 to 1931. Among them were the founder of the Bauhaus Walter

Gropius, Hans Scharoun who also participated in the master plan, Hugo Häring, Fred Forbát, and again Leberecht Migge who designed the open spaces. As in Frankfurt, building parts and floor plans were greatly standardized. Despite this, the architecture in Siemensstadt is more diverse, featuring such striking designs as Scharoun's 'Panzerkreuzer' ('battle ship' because of its dynamic, ship-like balconies and roofs). Gropius used brick surfaces to structure the long, flat-roofed blocks. Flats were generally small (mostly forty-eight square metres) but all had private bathrooms and balconies while sharing generous common facilities – roof terraces, kindergartens, health centres, shops, and even a district heating system, the first one in Berlin.

'Panzerkreuzer' by Hans Scharoun
Der so genannte Panzerkreuzer
von Hans Scharoun

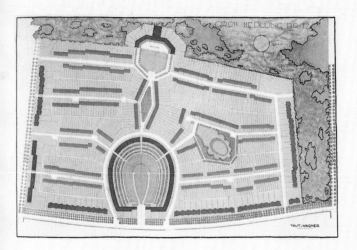

Bruno Taut **Hufeisensiedlung** **Berlin-Britz** **Germany** Deutschland **1925–1933**

Eine ähnliche Entwicklung nahm das Wohnungsprogramm in Berlin unter dem Baudirektor Martin Wagner. Dieser initiierte die Gründung einer gewerkschaftseigenen Baugesellschaft und beschäftigte sich erstmals mit Plattenbauweisen. Seine bekannteste Siedlung wurde die riesige Siemensstadt (1928–1931), an der auch Walter Gropius, Hans Scharoun, Hugo Häring und Fred Forbát beteiligt waren. Die Wohnungen waren klein (meist 48 Quadratmeter), wurden jedoch durch großzügige Gemeinschaftseinrichtungen und Dachterrassen ergänzt. Ähnlich beeindruckend ist die Siedlung in Berlin-Britz mit der großartigen Hufeisensiedlung von Bruno Taut.

Another impressive housing estate was erected in Berlin-Britz. The masterplan was by Martin Wagner and Bruno Taut, most buildings however being designed by Taut only. Compared to the Siemensstadt complex, Britz has a more suburban character with three-storey terraced houses dominating. Taut and Wagner favoured industrialized building production which – although not cheaper at that time – enabled construction to be completed faster.[6] Floor plans were strictly standardized resulting in only four types for more than 1,000 units. However, due to Taut's lively colour schemes, various window formats, front gardens, and alternating entrances the architecture is far from monotonous. Taut also used curved streets to create a more diverse impression which culminates in the stupendous Hufeisensiedlung (the 'horseshoe' shaped estate). From 1925 to 1933 Taut built more than 10,000 flats making him a true pioneer of social housing worldwide.

Central courtyard within the horseshoe-shaped complex
Innenhof des hufeisenförmigen Baus

Ernst May, Mart Stam   Magnitogorsk   Russia Russland   1929–1931

Unlike in the Netherlands, Austria and Germany, innovative architecture in France was seldom connected to social housing in the 1920s and 1930s. Among the few estates which took up the International Style in their formal repertoire is the Cité de la Muette at Drancy, built for the Département Seine public housing office by the architects Eugène Beaudouin and Marcel Lods in 1931 to 1934. The apartments were tiny (twenty-nine square metres for a one bedroom flat and kitchen), and the up-to-date building technology – steel skeleton, pre-fabricated, reinforced concrete elements for the façades, balconies and staircases[7] – further reduced the costs in order to comply with the strict budgets for social housing. The five, fifteen-storey towers nevertheless show surprisingly high architectural and urban qualities. To somehow compensate the limited space flats were equipped with the latest technology, including built-in wardrobes and central heating. The two architects planned similar housing projects on the outskirts of Paris (Suresnes, Clichy, Bagneux), and Lods later cooperated with Le Corbusier.

In the early 1930s the Soviet Union invited several prominent European architects – among them emigrants from Nazi Germany – to participate in the huge building programme which was part of an industrialization policy. While the revolutionary enthusiasm of the 1920s collective housing projects had already given way to more traditional models the task to design whole new cities in the eastern regions of the country must still have been tempting. The concept of the collective house was now replaced by the 'Sozgorod' collective housing areas[8] with large numbers of standardized dwellings situated around the necessary, social infrastructure-related facilities and near to industrial complexes. Urban planning and housing had become topics of scientific interest based on ratio and statistics rather than artistic expression. Thus, architects like Ernst May and Mart Stam worked on masterplans for new cities like Magnitogorsk, Leninsk and Kusnezk together with the Soviet architects Ginsburg, Milinis and others. Margarete Schütte-Lihotzky developed plans for standardized kindergartens.[9] The city of Magnitogorsk where construction had started in 1929, was to become the show piece of Soviet city planning, and (at least for some years) a laboratory for industrialized construction methods, though more and more hampered by the lack of appropriate building materials as well as by bureaucracy. Today, it may be seen as the last expression of the optimistic – or perhaps naïve – Neues Bauen approach to solving the most urgent challenges in the area of human settlement; given other economic and political conditions it could well have served as a model for the future.

6 see: www.gehag.de, 2005, p. 2
7 Benevolo, vol. 2, 1978, p. 214
8 Chan-Magomedow, p. 334
9 Noever (ed.), 1993, pp. 138–65

Eugène Beaudouin, Marcel Lods   Cité de la Muette   Drancy   France Frankreich   1931–1934

Frankreich hatte im Unterschied zu den Niederlanden, Österreich und Deutschland kaum innovative Architektur im sozialen Wohnungsbau zu bieten. Hier stellte die **Cité de la Muette** (1931–1934) in Drancy von **Eugène Beaudouin** und **Marcel Lods** mit ihren 15-stöckigen Türmen unter Verwendung vorgefertigter Betonelemente eine bemerkenswerte Ausnahme dar. Anfang der 1930er-Jahre schließlich zog es zahlreiche Architekten – darunter **Ernst May**, **Mart Stam** und **Margarete Schütte-Lihotzky** – in die **Sowjetunion**, wo komplette Industriestädte unter Anwendung wissenschaftlicher Planungsmethoden neu errichtet wurden. Besonders die neue Stadt **Magnitogorsk** war einige Jahre lang ein Labor für industrialisiertes Bauen, doch Materialmangel und Bürokratie behinderten zunehmend die Umsetzung der engagierten Planungen.

CITÉ INDUSTRIELLE

Tony Garnier
Etats-Unis
Lyons Lyon   France Frankreich   1920–1934

The Lyons born architect Tony Garnier caused a scandal when he presented his project for an industrial city, built of concrete, steel and glass, to the Prix de Rome jury in 1901. This first plan, later to be further developed into the famous Cité Industrielle project (1918), was based on his conviction that "antique architecture was an error. Only the truth is beautiful."[1] And truth was to be achieved by "satisfying the known needs by known means." Garnier's cité industrielle was in fact a radical break with academic city planning, as – for the first time – the ideal city was to be clearly structured into different zones for housing,

education, sports, administration, hospitals, and manufacturing purposes, making it a predecessor of the Athens charter. City planning was to be more a scientific task than an artistic one. Housing areas were to be complimented by shops, laundries, primary schools, etc., and should consist of one to three-storey houses surrounded by lush green areas. Garnier also laid down concrete rules for the housing estates which reflect the high priority given to health matters: at least one room of each flat should face south, inner courtyards should be forbidden, walls and floors should be of smooth materials with rounded corners.

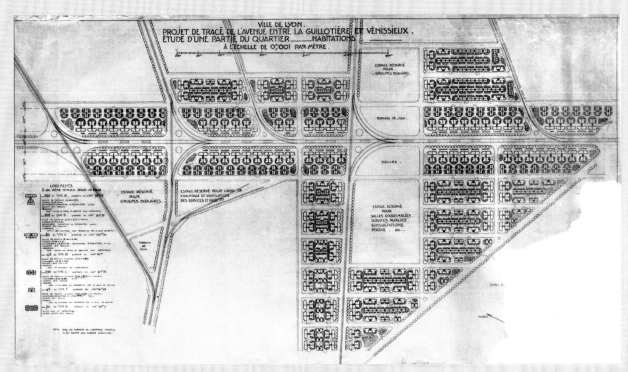

Tony Garnier's initial design, 1917 Tony Garniers erster Entwurf von 1917

The ideal city would have about 35,000 inhabitants. As a follower of Utopian Socialism and strongly influenced by Emile Zola, Garnier supposed that all land would in the future belong to the public, and this would facilitate rational planning based solely on human needs.

Surprisingly, the architect had the possibility of realizing his 'utopian' ideas – or at least partly. Édouard Herriot, the dynamic socialist mayor of Lyons, commissioned Garnier with the Grands Travaux (the large public buildings), including an abattoir, the famous Grange-Blanche Hospital, the Gerland stadium, and the impressive market hall (today Halle Tony Garnier). This, of course, was not the 'ideal' new city he had envisaged as the buildings were part of an existing urban fabric, but in 1920 Garnier had the chance to plan a whole new urban area along a boulevard almost five kilometres long, with about 5,000 housing units. The architect adapted his cité industrielle concept to this situation, placing three to five-storey blocks together with schools and other infrastructure-related buildings in a garden-like setting. Economic difficulties forced him to change this plan several times; in the end, only 1,563 apartments were built, and almost none of the public buildings. Nevertheless, the residential buildings of the Etats-Unis district – now with six storeys – demonstrate the uncompromising modernity of Garnier's con-

cept. All flats of this first low-cost (HLM) housing estate in France have balconies facing the extensive gardens which are designed very carefully, with benches, pedestrian walks, and pergolas. Façades are flat and simply structured with concrete balconies. The estate is characterized by an entirely new relationship of each part to the whole; there is nothing of the strictly modernist repertoire of the International Style as in contemporary German or Dutch estates but rather a timeless, humanistic approach to city planning.

The Etats-Unis complex became a synonym for socially oriented planning, and it also became extremely popular among its – low-income – residents. Thus, when in the 1980s many of the French social housing areas became centres of poverty and crime with the buildings deteriorating, the Lyons tenants took a more optimistic view. Together with the housing association they organized the refurbishment of their estate, including the stunning project of the Musée Urbain Tony Garnier. This 'museum', created by a number of artists from around the world, consists of huge murals depicting Garnier's cité industrielle drawings on the fire walls of the residential blocks. The pioneering Etats-Unis estate thus received national attention for a second time.

1 Piessat, 1988

Der aus Lyon stammende Architekt Tony Garnier hatte 1901 für den Prix de Rome eine Industriestadt aus Beton, Stahl und Glas eingereicht und damit für einen Skandal gesorgt. Der Entwurf stellte einen radikalen Bruch mit der akademischen Stadtplanung dar: Zum ersten Mal sollte die ideale Stadt in Zonen für Wohnen, Erziehung, Sport, Verwaltung, Krankenhäuser und Produktion gegliedert werden – ein Vorläufer der Charta von Athen. Nach Garniers Plänen sollten hygienische Überlegungen den Wohnungsbau bestimmen: Ausrichtung der Wohnräume nach Süden, Verbot aller Innenhöfe, in den Wohnungen Oberflächen aus weichen Materialien mit abgerundeten Ecken. Garnier, ein Anhänger des Utopischen Sozialismus, ging dabei vom öffentlichen Eigentum an Grund und Boden aus.

Ab 1920 erhielt Garnier die Möglichkeit, zumindest einen Teil seiner Ideen in Lyon zu realisieren, zunächst mit öffentlichen Bauten wie dem berühmten Krankenhaus Grange-Blanche, später mit dem komplett neuen Stadtviertel Etats-Unis. Obwohl hier statt der vorgesehenen 5000 nur 1563 Wohnungen errichtet wurden und ein Großteil der geplanten öffentlichen Bauten den wirtschaftlichen Schwierigkeiten zum Opfer fiel, zeigte sich Garniers Meisterschaft in der modernen, aber niemals dogmatischen Architektur der sechsgeschossigen Wohnblöcke und ihrer Einbettung in überaus sorgfältig geplante Grünbereiche. Das Wohnviertel Etats-Unis wurde zum Synonym sozial orientierter Planung. Im Gegensatz zu vielen französischen Sozialsiedlungen blieb es auch später von Verfall und Kriminalität verschont. In den 1980er-Jahren realisierte die Wohnungsbaugesellschaft gemeinsam mit den Mietern das Musée Urbain Tony Garnier. Zeichnungen der Cité industrielle wurden auf den Feuermauern der Wohnblöcke ins Riesenhafte vergrößert und machten den Pioniercharakter der Siedlung zum zweiten Mal deutlich.

Brinkmann & van der Vlugt, Willem van Tijen   Bergpolder   Rotterdam   The Netherlands Niederlande   1933–1934

Maxwell Fry   Kensal House   London   Great Britain Großbritannien   1936

The idea of a planned industrial city was not new to England, of course, where socially-oriented urban planning had started with projects like Saltaire in the 19th century. In the 1930s, however, housing policies were far less advanced than in continental Europe, and social housing was often left to progressive-minded industrialists. With Kensal House at Ladbroke Grove in West London, Maxwell Fry, a co-founder of the British CIAM affiliate MARS, realized an outstanding example of low-cost housing for a gas company, in 1936. Planned to re-house former slum dwellers its elegantly curving blocks contain sixty-eight spacious apartments accompanied by a community centre, a laundry, a restaurant, a kindergarten and a crèche. Each flat has two balconies and all living rooms enjoy direct sunlight. Fry understood this estate as a prototype for 'urban villages' which would provide the working class with affordable houses in a healthy environment. The reformatory aspect is also expressed by the modernist architecture with flat roofs and white façades, structured into groups by the balconies.

In the Netherlands, where city planning was still influenced by the groundbreaking works of Hendrik Petrus Berlage, new housing production, though more and more industrialized, was usually conceived as part of urban development. Thus, the integration of shops and other social infrastructure facilities was common practice; what was new in the 1930s was the intense search for a new relation between the private and the public space. This, together with cost-reduction brought about by standardization and industrial building methods, led to some of the most remarkable housing projects of pre-WW II Europe. At the Bergpolder apartment building in Rotterdam the architects' office Brinkmann & van der Vlugt with Willem van Tijen established a new high-rise typology: a long rectangular block with completely identical flats along an open access gallery. This semi-private space seems to redefine the traditional residential streets of small Dutch towns with their sensible territorial-related concept of space.[2] Although kitchens and bedrooms open directly to the gallery the plan was thus based on an accepted cultural model and became very popular in post-war Dutch housing. The advantages were clear: All flats could be oriented to two sides; industrialization and standardization were enhanced; floor plans were flexible; and, for the first time, the larger number of dwellings made elevators affordable in low-cost workers' housing. Bergpolder shows functionalist architecture in its original sense: un-dogmatic, open to existing and to new spatial needs, yet sensitive in its response to the built environment. The architects provided a model for the industrial city of the 20th century – stylistically very different from Garnier's cité industrielle but close in regard to its societal aims.

2   Grinberg, 1982, pp. 125, 126

In England waren seit dem 19. Jahrhundert neue Industriestädte wie zum Beispiel Saltaire errichtet worden, doch blieb bis in die 1930er-Jahre sozialer Wohnungsbau der Initiative einiger fortschrittlicher Unternehmer überlassen. Ein außergewöhnlich qualitätsvolles Projekt wurde vom Architekten **Maxwell Fry** 1936 in Ladbroke Grove im Westen Londons geplant: **Kensal House**, eine Wohnanlage mit umfangreichen Gemeinschaftseinrichtungen für ehemalige Slumbewohner. In den **Niederlanden**, wo seit den Planungen von Hendrik Petrus Berlage Wohnungsbau als Teil einer umfassenden Stadtentwicklung verstanden wurde, führten Experimente mit Standardisierung und industriellen Baumethoden zu bemerkenswerten Anlagen wie **Bergpolder** in Rotterdam von **Brinkmann & van der Vlugt** mit **Willem van Tijen**. Hier wurde die Intimität traditioneller holländischer Wohnstraßen durch den Laubengang neu interpretiert. Erstmals gab es auch im sozialen Wohnungsbau Aufzüge und flexible Grundrisse. Bergpolder lieferte ein Modell für den Wohnungsbau des 20. Jahrhunderts – stilistisch verschieden von Ganiers Cité industrielle, aber sehr ähnlich im gesellschaftlichen Anspruch.

LIBERATED HOUSING   BEFREITES WOHNEN

Ludwig Mies van der Rohe, Le Corbusier
Weissenhofsiedlung
Stuttgart   Germany Deutschland   1927

In 1925, Ludwig Mies van der Rohe was commissioned by the German Werkbund to develop a concept for a housing exhibition in Stuttgart to take place in 1927. This included the master plan with terraces following the hilly terrain, and the selection of seventeen architects from the Netherlands (J. J. P. Oud, Mart Stam), Belgium (Victor Bourgeois), Germany (Adolf Gustav Schneck, Peter Behrens, Hans Scharoun, Walter Gropius, Ludwig Hilberseimer, Bruno Taut, Max Taut, Hans Poelzig, Richard Döcker, Adolf Rading, and himself, Ludwig Mies van der Rohe), Austria (Josef Frank) and Switzerland (Le Corbusier, Pierre Jeanneret). Mies did not intervene in their architecture except in the case of the obligatory flat roofs. The choice of the site for this coordinated demonstration of modernism was not coincidental, as the 'Stuttgart School of Architecture' was dominated by traditionalist architects like Paul Bonatz and Paul Schmitthenner who strongly opposed the Werkbund exhibition. A conflict was certainly to be expected and the flat cubes of the Weissenhofsiedlung were promptly dubbed 'Arab village' or a 'suburb of Jerusalem'.[1] As a consequence, its 'un-Germanic' archi-

tecture was severely altered from 1933 onwards. While most of the architects presented either small villas (Frank, Scharoun, Poelzig, Döcker, Schneck) which obviously did not aim at standardization, or prototypes for terraced housing (Oud, Stam), the buildings by Behrens, Mies van der Rohe, and Le Corbusier focussed on multi-level urban housing. Among them Mies' own design followed the principles of functionalism more than any other Weissenhof building. Dominating the whole area the long, four-storey block represents a radical break with traditional urban planning concepts in which housing was arranged around inner courtyards. Instead, all flats are orientated to two sides. No hierarchy being displayed on the façades which are structured by the staircases and by the balconies, the block could easily be extended, or repeated on any other site and, probably most importantly, the steel skeleton construction allowed flexible floor plans. Volumes, exterior walls, and statics are treated completely separately, transferring the model of the modern office building onto a housing project for the first time. Mies also developed a system of light timber elements for interior walls.

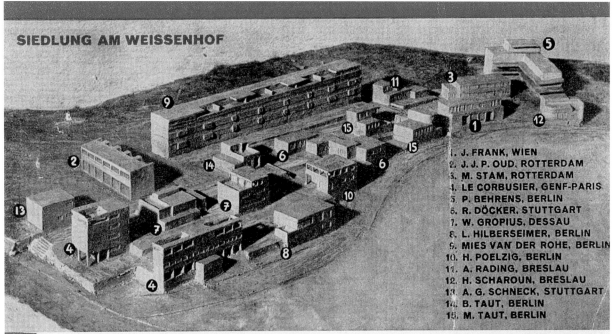

SIEDLUNG AM WEISSENHOF

1. J. FRANK, WIEN
2. J. J. P. OUD, ROTTERDAM
3. M. STAM, ROTTERDAM
4. LE CORBUSIER, GENF-PARIS
5. P. BEHRENS, BERLIN
6. R. DÖCKER, STUTTGART
7. W. GROPIUS, DESSAU
8. L. HILBERSEIMER, BERLIN
9. MIES VAN DER ROHE, BERLIN
10. H. POELZIG, BERLIN
11. A. RADING, BRESLAU
12. H. SCHAROUN, BRESLAU
13. A. G. SCHNECK, STUTTGART
14. B. TAUT, BERLIN
15. M. TAUT, BERLIN

ERSTELLT DURCH DIE STADT STUTTGART NACH DEN VORSCHLÄGEN DES DEUTSCHEN WERKBUNDES

WERKBUND AUSSTELLUNG **DIE WOHNUNG**
JULI-SEPT. 1927 **STUTTGART**

With the exception of kitchens and bathrooms, none of the rooms have any specific size or function – or rather, they can be adapted to any function needed at a given time. Perhaps, more than any other building, Mies' Weissenhof residential block explains the enthusiasm of Befreites Wohnen (Liberated Housing) as expressed by the CIAM General Secretary Siegfried Giedion.[2]

Der Deutsche Werkbund beauftragte Ludwig Mies van der Rohe mit der Planung einer Wohnungsbauausstellung in Stuttgart im Jahr 1927. Mies entwarf den terrassenförmig angelegten Bebauungsplan und war auch für die Auswahl der 17 Architekten verantwortlich. Flachdächer waren verbindlich vorgeschrieben. Der Konflikt mit der konservativen Stuttgarter Architekturschule war damit vorprogrammiert: Die Weißenhofsiedlung wurde als »arabisches Dorf« und »Vorort von Jerusalem« verunglimpft.

Die meisten Architekten planten kleine, für Standardisierung kaum geeignete Villen oder Prototypen für Reihenhäuser. Peter Behrens, Mies van der Rohe und Le Corbusier setzten dagegen auf mehrgeschossigen Wohnungsbau, wobei vor allem Mies' eigenes Gebäude die Prinzipien des Funktionalismus verkörpert. Der langgestreckte Block bricht radikal mit der üblichen Rasterbauweise mit geschlossenem Innenhof. Alle Wohnungen sind zweiseitig orientiert, die Fassade zeigt keinerlei Hierarchie und wird lediglich durch die Balkone und Treppenhäuser strukturiert. Vor allem aber erlaubte die Stahlskelettkonstruktion erstmals flexible Wohnungsgrundrisse. Die Funktion der Räume ist daher nicht festgelegt, wodurch das Schlagwort des CIAM-Generalsekretärs Siegfried Giedion vom »befreiten Wohnen« hier reale Bedeutung bekommt.

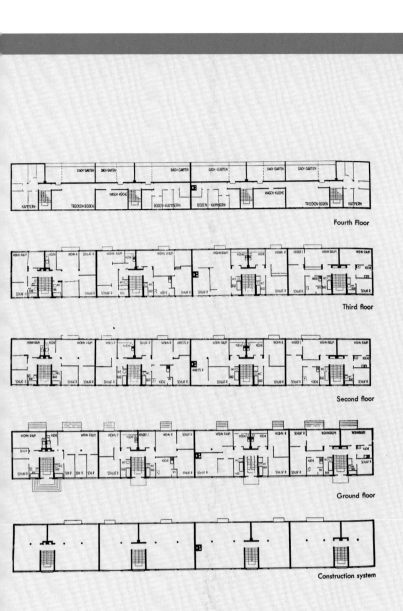

Fourth Floor

Third floor

Second floor

Ground floor

Construction system

Multi-storey apartment building by Mies van der Rohe
Geschosswohnungsbau von Mies van der Rohe

49

Le Corbusier, at this time already a famous architect, designed a detached and semi-detached building for Stuttgart, working together with his cousin Pierre Jeanneret. Like in the Mies building a steel skeleton offers a free spatial concept based on the 'five principles' developed earlier for the Citrohan House: construction on pillars (pilotis), roof terraces, open floor plans, open façades and horizontal wall-to-wall strip windows. Interior walls, as far as they exist at all, are partly rounded or have irregular shapes contributing to a dynamic flow of volumes. As a consequence, the rooms appear much larger than they actually are. In fact, space is relatively limited, especially in the case of the 'infamously' narrow corridor which caused some irritation during the exhibition.[3] The reference to a train carriage is further enhanced by foldaway beds in the living room.

Although similar to Mies in some of the basic design principles Le Corbusier's Weissenhof buildings are far less rooted in the severe, formal repertoire of the German Bauhaus. The shading of the roof terrace seems to grow out of the lateral façades thus contributing dramatically to the plasticity of the building. Also, unlike many other modernist architects, Le Corbusier favoured a lively colour scheme.

1 Hammerbacher, 2002, p. 16
2 Giedion, 1929
3 Le Corbusier in: Das neue Frankfurt, 1928, pp. 11–15

Le Corbusier entwarf gemeinsam mit Pierre Jeanneret zwei Stahl-skelettbauten, die seine früher formulierten »Fünf Punkte zu einer neuen Architektur« verdeutlichen: Errichtung der Bauten auf Pfeilern (pilotis), Dachterrassen, freie Grundrissgestaltung, freie Fassadengestaltung, Fensterbänder. Trotz äußerst bescheidener Ausmaße – besonders der extrem schmale Korridor im ersten Obergeschoss des Zweifamilienhauses erregte die Ausstellungsbesucher – erscheinen die Wohnungen durch den freien Raumfluss geräumig. Insgesamt ist Le Corbusiers Planung weniger dem strengen Formenkanon des Neuen Bauens verpflichtet als der Wohnblock von Mies van der Rohe. Die Häuser zeichnen sich durch Plastizität und lebhafte Farbgebung aus.

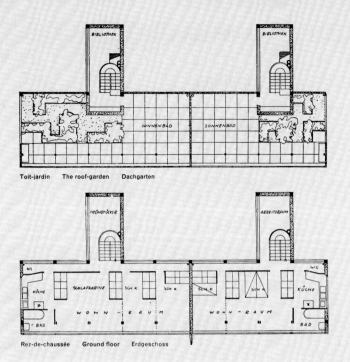

Toit-jardin   The roof-garden   Dachgarten

Rez-de-chaussée   Ground floor   Erdgeschoss

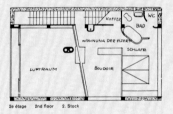

2e étage   2nd floor   2. Stock

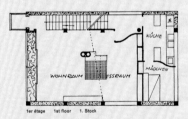

1er étage   1st floor   1. Stock

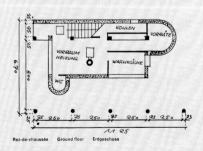

Rez-de-chaussée   Ground floor   Erdgeschoss

Semi-detached building (above) and
detached building (below) by Le Corbusier
Zweifamilienhaus (oben) und
Einfamilienhaus (unten) von Le Corbusier

Werkbundsiedlung Vienna Wien Austria Österreich 1932

Buildings by Gerrit Rietveld (top) and Adolf Loos (above)
Wohnhäuser von Gerrit Rietveld (oben) und Adolf Loos (unten)

The attention that the Weissenhof estate received internationally led the Austrian Werkbund to organize a similar building exhibition at the Vienna Werkbundsiedlung in 1932 under its president Josef Frank. Due however to the economic crisis and the rise of fascism this exhibition proved far less successful. Furthermore, Frank excluded all architects who had participated in Stuttgart (except himself) and insisted on low-rise buildings. Some of the houses (Frank, Oskar Strnad, Richard Neutra) resemble villas rather than prototypes for new social housing which the City of Vienna had expected. Conversely, others provided a high-quality living environment in spite of very limited space, especially in the case of Gerrit Rietveld who repeated the split-level scheme of his Utrecht Erasmuslaan terraced houses. The most striking design, however, came from Adolf Loos, who for the first time transferred his multi-dimensional Raumplan spatial concept from luxurious villas onto working class housing.

Nach dem Vorbild der Stuttgarter Ausstellung wurden Werkbundsiedlungen in Wien (1932, unter der Gesamtleitung von Josef Frank mit innovativen Lösungen vor allem von Gerrit Rietveld und Adolf Loos), Breslau (1929), Zürich-Neubühl (1928–1932), Stockholm (1930) und Prag (1928–1940) errichtet.

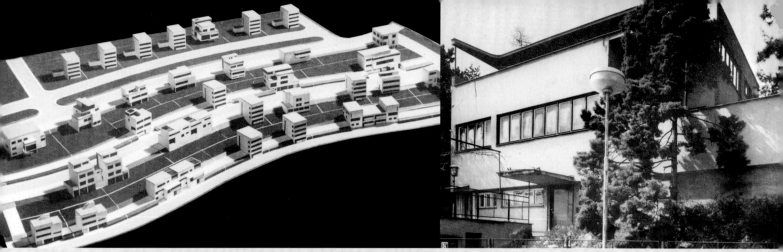

Pavel Janak **Baba Estate** Siedlung Baba **Prague** Prag **Czech Republic** Tschechische Republik **1928–1940**

Family villas by František Kerhart (above right)
and Mart Stam (below)
Wohnhäuser von František Kerhart (oben rechts)
und Mart Stam (unten)

Other housing exhibitions were held by the national Werkbund organisations at Breslau/Wroclav (1929), Zurich-Neubühl (1928–32), and Stockholm (1930). The Prague Baba Estate (1928–40), unlike the Stuttgart and Vienna developments, was not financed by the municipality. Instead, private builders chose their architects from the Czechoslovak Werkbund members, with Mart Stam being the only foreign architect invited.[4] The master plan by Pavel Janak follows the Stuttgart example, with flat roofs prescribed as obligatory. Today, the Baba Estate still proves the strikingly high quality which Czech modernist architecture had reached in the 1920s. The Weissenhof Exhibition also led to the founding of CIAM (Congrès Internationaux d'Architecture Moderne) in 1928 which held its second conference in 1929 under the heading 'Housing for an existential minimum'

Alfred Roth, Emil Roth, Marcel Breuer   Doldertal Residences Doldertal-Häuser   **Zurich** Zürich   **Switzerland** Schweiz   **1936**

In Switzerland Alfred Roth, who had already worked with Le Corbusier and had participated in the Zurich-Neubühl Werkbund estate, built one of the showpieces of International Style architecture together with his cousin Emil Roth and with Marcel Breuer. The Doldertal Residences (1936), three multi-occupation buildings erected for an affluent clientele – among them the CIAM General Secretary Siegfried Giedion[5] – in a superb location, not only influenced Swiss architecture over the next few years but became internationally known through Giedion's publications. Roth succeeded in transforming the modernist vocabulary – skeletal frame construction, white walls, flat roofs, pilotis (supporting columns), flush windows – into a succession of floating interior and exterior spaces. In its plasticity the building extends the tectonic order of Bauhaus architecture while redeveloping its main achievements – transparency and open floor plans.

In Zürich planten die Architekten **Alfred Roth, Emil Roth** und **Marcel Breuer** mit den **Doldertal-Häusern** 1936 herausragende Wohnhäuser des Neuen Bauens, bei denen Innen- und Außenräume zu einem fließenden Kontinuum werden. In **Mailand** schuf **Giuseppe Terragni** mit der **Casa Rustici** am noblen Corso Sempione ein Gebäude, dessen wahre Bedeutung erst nach dem Zweiten Weltkrieg bewusst wurde. Terragni verband den Internationalen Stil mit regionalen Elementen und spielte virtuos mit Transparenz und Geschlossenheit, mit Licht und Schatten.

Giuseppe Terragni Casa Rustici Milan Mailand Italy Italien 1933–1936

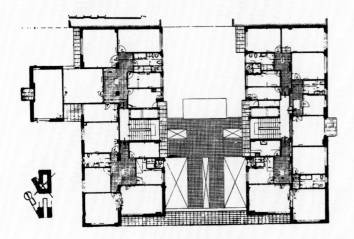

Among the modern architects who were closely involved in housing design Giuseppe Terragni is one of the most outstanding. He had already gained national attention as part of the famous 'gruppo 7' team of architects for 'rational architecture'[6] when he was commissioned to plan Casa Rustici in Milan's famed Corso Sempione. It is probably the most important contribution to modernist planning in an existing urban context. While carefully respecting the scale of the neighbouring 19th-century blocks, the building is open to the boulevard. However, by connecting the two parallel wings by large balconies Terragni introduces a poetic play with transparent and closed volumes, with light and shadow, with tradition and innovation, with regionalism and internationalism. This play was soon to be forcibly interrupted but was taken up again – under very different circumstances – by Italian, post-war housing programmes.

4 Kohout, 2004, pp. 134–39
5 Benevolo, vol. 2, 1978, p. 283
6 Fonatti, 1987, p. 23

COLLECTIVE LIVING   KOLLEKTIVES WOHNEN

Moisei Ginzburg, Ignatii Milinis
Narkomfin Apartment Building   Wohnblock Narkomfin
Moscow Moskau   **Russia** Russland   **1928–1930**

The Soviet Union organized a number of competitions to develop new models of collective housing in the early 1920s. While conditions for such buildings remained more or less the same – small individual units, complemented by communal facilities like crèches, kindergartens, baths, libraries and restaurants – their architecture developed from traditional vernacular forms to daring constructivist projects. Leading constructivist architects, notably Konstantin Melnikov, presented plans which included a separate wing with kitchen, restaurant, kindergarten, etc., connected to the residential block via a glazed corridor on the second level. Other projects were based on a gallery system which was to become a common model for collective housing: a broad corridor – or rather an internal street, a feature taken up later by Le Corbusier in his 'unités d'habitation' – connecting the dwellings with the communal facilities. Among the architects participating in these competitions were El Lissitzky and the Vesnin brothers.

None of these early projects, however, were ever built. It was only in 1927 when the OSA (Organisation of Modern Architects) announced another competition, based on the standardized floor plan types produced by the State Committee for Construction, that a number of projects were realized. The architects Moisei Ginzburg and Ignatii Milinis presented a strikingly modern complex for 1,100 residents consisting of two blocks: a long rectangular six-storey residential unit with a rooftop terrace, and a lower block containing the communal infrastructure (library, dining room, club, meeting room). All apartments had individual bathrooms and extended over two or three levels. Thus, a corridor – again designed as a street-like semi-public space for multiple use – was needed only on every second level. This internal system was adopted and further developed by Le Corbusier in the 1940s, omitting however the natural lighting feature which Ginzburg and Milinis introduced through the generous use of glazed walls.

The architecture of the Narkomfin Complex is pure functionalism, with details like the handrails being designed very carefully. The residential block stands on pillars and is characterized by the enormous length of the horizontal strip windows; in sharp contrast, the façades of the communal building are completely glazed. Housing standards were relatively high, given the economic circumstances of the Soviet Union at that time, including well-equipped bathrooms and central heating. The

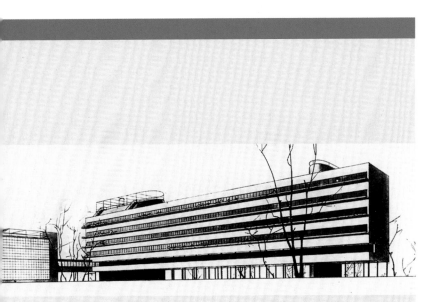

architects argued that with mass production such standards would become affordable to all citizens. This did not help, however. Collective housing was more and more seen as too expensive and the organization of living space 'too unclear',[1] until it was officially forbidden in 1932.[2] Nevertheless, not only the impressive buildings but the idea itself survived. It came up again in some Soviet projects in the 1970s and, in the meantime, it was redesigned on a much smaller scale in various countries, particularly in Czechoslovakia, Denmark and Sweden.

1 Chan-Magomedow, 1983, p. 347
2 Museum für Gestaltung, Zurich, 1987, p. 32

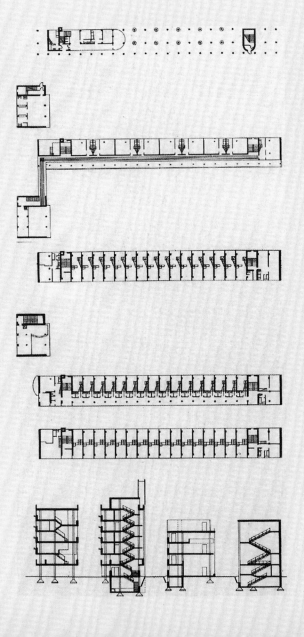

In der Sowjetunion fand in den 1920er-Jahren ein Reihe von Wettbewerben für neue kollektive Wohnformen statt. Die Grundkonzeption blieb gleich – kleine Wohneinheiten mit Gemeinschaftseinrichtungen –, die Architektur entwickelte sich jedoch von traditionellen Formen zu kühnen konstruktivistischen Projekten weiter. Einige Elemente wurden konstitutiv für alle Kollektivwohnhäuser, etwa der breite Gang, eigentlich eine interne Straße, wie ihn auch Le Corbusier später in seinen Unités d'Habitation verwendete. 1927 veranstaltete die OSA (Vereinigung moderner Architekten) einen weiteren Wettbewerb, für den Moisei Ginzburg und Ignatii Milinis einen kompromisslos modernen Entwurf vorlegten. Der realisierte Bau besteht aus einem langen, sechsstöckigen Wohntrakt mit Dachterrasse und einem niedrigeren Gebäude mit den Gemeinschaftseinrichtungen wie Bibliothek, Speisesaal, Club, Versammlungsraum. Die Wohnungen sind mehrgeschossig, wodurch nur auf jeder zweiten Ebene ein Gang benötigt wird. Die Architektur des Narkomfin-Wohnblocks ist purer Funktionalismus, mit Baukörpern auf Stützen, Glaswänden und Fensterbändern. Durch Standardisierung sollten die hochwertigen Wohnungen allgemein erschwinglich werden, doch wurden weitere Kollektivhäuser 1932 offiziell verboten. Erst später wurden ähnliche Konzepte, vor allem in der Tschechoslowakei, in Dänemark und Schweden, wieder aufgenommen.

Swedish architecture gradually shifted from classicism to functionalism in the early 1930s. At the same time, the question of housing gained in importance and leading architects had concerned themselves with it.[3] This included new approaches to overall urban planning as well as to experimental housing. In 1935, Sven Markelius, who had already designed some of Sweden's most outstanding buildings, devised a collective housing unit in John Ericssongatan in Stockholm. Obviously influenced by the earlier Soviet ideas of collective housing, as well as by projects in Germany, Austria and Switzerland – the so-called *Einküchenhäuser*[4] or one kitchen buildings – and supported by the Swedish Womens' Movement, Markelius designed a number of different collective housing units. Only the Erissonsgatan building, however, was to be realized. The fifty-five flats – with one, two or three bedrooms – were complemented by a range of communal facilities: the central restaurant (which replaced individual kitchens but was also open to visitors), a children's playroom, a toddlers' room, and a separate unit for sick children. Markelius wanted to bring children in contact with people outside their families, and he also took great care of the toys to be provided in the children's rooms and in the playground designed for the communal courtyard. Residents should be freed from conventional household chores through the use of cleaning services (i.e. laundry could simply be thrown into a chute connected to the central laundry unit), the installation of waste-disposal systems, and service-lifts connected to the restaurant, etc. Although, obviously, only better-situated tenants could afford such comforts (among them the radical intellectual élite of the time[5]), most of the central services still function today. The architecture towards the street is characterized by protruding, saw-like balconies and by the generous glazed entrance hall.

One of the most interesting collective housing units – Kolektivni Dum – was built by Jiří Voženílek in Zlín,[6] Czechoslovakia, in 1950. It was part of the huge construction programme in this city which had been founded by the Bata Shoe Company in the 1920s and had become a true laboratory of modernist architecture involving, among others, Le Corbusier.

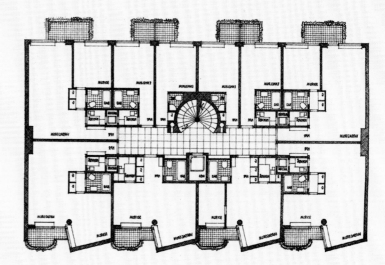

Beeinflusst von den sowjetischen Planungen und den ›Einküchenhäusern‹ in Deutschland, Österreich und der Schweiz errichtete **Sven Markelius** 1935 das **Kollektivhaus** in der **John Ericssongatan** in **Stockholm**. Die 55 Wohnungen verfügen über noch heute funktionierende Gemeinschaftseinrichtungen wie eine Zentralküche mit Speiseaufzügen, Kinder- und Säuglingsräume, Krankenraum und eine Zentralwäscherei mit Wäscheabwurfschacht in jeder Wohnung. Damit war das Projekt aber nur für Gutverdienende erschwinglich. Architektonisch prägend sind die sägeblattartigen Balkongruppen an der Straßenseite.

Zu den interessantesten Kollektivwohnhäusern gehört das **Kolektivni Dum** (1950) von **Jiří Voženílek** in **Zlín** in der Tschechischen Republik, der vom Schuhfabrikanten Bata in den 1930er-Jahren gegründeten modernen Stadt.

3   Lindvall, 1992, p. 72
4   Museum für Gestaltung, Zurich, 1987, pp. 29–31
5   Andersson, 1997, p. 130
6   Novak, 1993, pp. 72–77

THE WHITE CITY   DIE WEISSE STADT

Arne Jacobsen
Bellavista Residences   *Wohnanlage Bellavista*
Klampenborg, Copenhagen *Kopenhagen*   **Denmark** *Dänemark*   **1931–1934**

The Bellavista housing estate is part of a large urban development along Strandvejen – the coastal road north of Copenhagen. The architect Arne Jacobsen had previously been working on a number of projects in Klampenborg, including the award-winning – though never implemented – plan for the Danish National Museum (1928). In 1931 he won the competition for the Klampenborg Beach Club which was to become one of the proponents of the International Style in Scandinavia. Later buildings include the famous Bellevue Theatre (1935) and the Texaco Gas Station with its stunning circular projecting roof supported by a single column.[1]

The housing estate, commissioned by three local developers in 1931, was to become the core of the Bellevue area as well as one of Jacobsen's masterpieces. Local building regulations were actually favourable towards modern architecture. The height of the buildings was strictly limited which encouraged flat roofs, and all new buildings had to be white in order to harmonize with the surroundings, but Jacobsen also wanted to provide each of the sixty-eight apartments with an unspoilt view to the sea. This resulted in a U-shaped floor plan with two to three-storey wings encircling a large, green courtyard. Jacobsen's most important innovation, however, was to organize the parallel wings in a saw-like shape which gives each apartment a south-oriented balcony protected from the neighbours. Targeting at a more affluent clientele the apartments also offered a high standard, including private bathrooms, electric stoves, refrigerators, an automatic waste disposal system and a communal radio antenna.

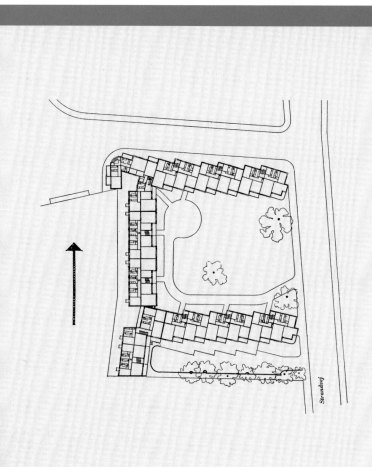

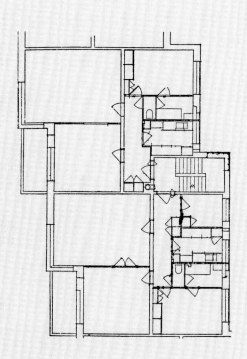

While the overall architectural form of the Bellavista Estate is reminiscent of the German Bauhaus style – in particular Gropius' Siemensstadt and May's Frankfurt housing projects – at the same time it shows a very personal 'Scandinavian' design approach which is more similar to Alvar Aalto's earlier buildings in Finland. In spite of the addition of the two lateral wings which, in theory, could be extended endlessly, the whole building is composed as a huge – yet inviting – sculpture responding to its built and natural environments. Thus it is clearly planned for a specific location rather than suggesting a prototype for ubiquitous 'housing machines', something many of the Bauhaus architects aimed at.

Details are particularly carefully designed; the corner balconies, for example, are rounded to provide a more inviting appearance from the street, staircases are directly lit by generous glass walls and additional, sculptural effects are achieved by the continuous play with shadows giving the Bellavista estate an almost Mediterranean appearance. According to Leonardo Benevolo this also proves that the International Style had a large variety of options to fulfil different needs, 'even the need for the picturesque' so highly estimated by the Nordic tradition.[2]

1 Thau, 2002, pp. 232–51
2 Benevolo, 1978, p. 275

Die Wohnhausanlage Bellavista bildet den Kern eines umfangreichen Neubaugebiets nördlich von Kopenhagen, wo Arne Jacobsen in den folgenden Jahren eine ganze Reihe aufsehenerregender Bauten errichtete. Die lokalen Bauvorschriften förderten moderne Architektur, da die Beschränkung der Bauhöhe flache Dächer nahe legte und alle Gebäude – im Hinblick auf ihre Umgebung – weiß sein sollten. Um allen 68 Wohnungen einen ungehinderten Blick auf das Meer zu ermöglichen, entwarf Jacobsen einen U-förmigen Baukörper mit zwei- bis dreigeschossigen Trakten, die sich um einen begrünten Hof gruppieren. Die sägezahnartige Anordnung der zwei parallelen Baukörper gibt jeder Wohnung einen vor Einblicken geschützten südorientierten Balkon. Da ein zahlungskräftiges Publikum angesprochen werden sollte, wurden alle Wohnungen mit einem für ihre Zeit hohen Standard ausgestattet – Badewannen, elektrische Herde, Kühlschränke, Müllabwurfsschächte und Gemeinschaftsantenne.

Die funktionalistische Architektur zeigt im Detail einen sehr persönlichen ›skandinavischen‹ Zugang, der an Alvar Aalto erinnert. Das Gebäude erscheint wie eine große Plastik, die in ihrem Spiel mit Licht und Schatten im Dialog mit der Natur steht. Für Leonardo Benevolo stellte dies den Beweis dar, dass der Internationale Stil unterschiedlichste Ansprüche erfüllen konnte – darunter auch jenen nach dem »Pittoresken, der von der nordischen Tradition so geschätzt wird«.

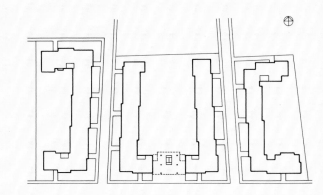

Arieh Sharon   Meneot Ovdim   Tel Aviv   Israel   1930

Arne Jacobsen' s personal interpretation of the International Style is best mirrored by the very specific approach to modernism undertaken under completely different climatic and cultural conditions – in Israel. In the 1930s, Tel Aviv received a great number of architects trained in Europe who participated in creating 'the largest urban ensemble of Modern Architecture ever built.'[3] They deliberately employed the International Style which had often been denounced as Jewish but which at the same time provided an 'architecture of hope'[4] with openly Western European origins for Palestine. The 1920s European architectural forms were thus redeveloped and adapted to the climatic extremes in the 1930. Newer European architecture, on the other hand, by architects like Le Corbusier, Richard Neutra, Giuseppe Terragni and others who tried to overcome the strict, formal repertoire of the Bauhaus, was not incorporated, partly because less professional ties existed to countries like France or Italy, and partly because the open floor plans of 1930s Befreites Bauen (liberated building) seemed less adaptable to a desert environment.

Naturally, housing was one of the focal points of new construction in Israel, mainly commissioned by the newly founded building associations. The rapid growth of Tel Aviv led to rather normative urban plans based on repetitive grid pattern schemes which, together with increasing land speculation, favoured massive, cubic blocks. While many of these buildings appear rather stern and uniform, larger housing estates like the Meneot Ovdim workers' flats commissioned by the General Trades Union Federa-

tion show a surprising degree of variety. Their architects, Josef Neufeld, Israel Dicker, Carl Rubin and Arieh Sharon, designed the large volumes around generous inner courtyards which are ventilated by gaps to the surrounding streets. This also gives the long façades a certain rhythm, as do the balconies and the staircases. Ironically, many of the formal elements – flat roofs, white walls, pergolas, flat façades, shade aprons, protruding concrete bands, flush windows, etc. – seem less alien to the oriental environment of Palestine than to the traditional European cityscape.[5] The plasticity of the White City as envisaged under Neues Bauen in Germany is thus best expressed in the grid pattern urban schemes of Tel Aviv.

3   Nerdinger, 1994, p. 7
4   Ibid., p. 9
5   Nerdinger, 1994, pp. 32–34

Überraschenderweise werden diese ›weißen Städte‹ unter ganz anderen klimatischen und kulturellen Bedingungen wieder aufgegriffen: in Israel. In Europa oft als ›jüdisch‹ denunziert, wurde der Internationale Stil in Palästina zur Architektur der Hoffnung. Zu den besten Bauten gehören die Arbeitersiedlungen in Meneot Ovdim, Tel Aviv, von Josef Neufeld, Israel Dicker, Carl Rubin und Arieh Sharon, die mit ihren langen flachen Fassaden, Bandfenstern, Sonnenblenden und Flachdächern in der orientalischen Umgebung vielleicht sogar weniger fremd wirkten als in Deutschland, dem Ursprungsland des Neuen Bauens.

ART DECO

Môrice Leroux
Gratte-Ciel
Villeurbanne, Lyons Lyon   France Frankreich   1927–1934

Some outstanding housing estates, it seems, are less known simply because they do not fit into mainstream architectural theory. This is certainly true of the Gratte-Ciel (skyscraper) housing complex at Villeurbanne, a Lyons suburb. Its architect, Môrice Leroux, was recommended by Tony Garnier who had built several remarkable buildings in Lyons himself. In fact, Leroux' plan can be seen as a successor of the utopian cité industrielle concept which Garnier had partly applied to his Etats-Unis area, an HLM (low-cost) housing project with surprisingly high standards, including all modern amenities like central heating and elevators. But Leroux was also fascinated by contemporary American architecture and he used American construction methods, filling a steel skeleton with bricks.

The residential buildings with some 1,500 flats are grouped in two parallel blocks, creating a strong counterpoint to the classicist Town Hall. The complex also includes the Palais de travail (Palace of Labour), a communal building containing a theatre, an indoor pool, meeting rooms for the unions and for workers' clubs, and an evening school proudly named the 'Proletarian University'. But it is the housing development which most strongly defines the urban space, dominated by the two symmetrical skyscrapers at the entrance to the central residential street. The towers are connected to linear ten-storey blocks where another stylistic element of contemporary American high-rise architecture has been adopted: the upper levels are stepped back, creating spacious private terraces. Although Antonio Sant'Elia envisaged such terraces in his futurist city design in 1914, this element is also genuinely French. Henri Sauvage had already included such designs in his utopian projects and had realized it on a smaller scale in the residential buildings in the Rue Vavin (1912) and Rue des Amiraux (1922), both in Paris. Higher buildings could thus be constructed in narrow streets, according to respective building regulations. This however also became one of the distinctive stylistic features of Art Deco architecture, particularly in France.

Art Deco elements can be found on the entrance doors, on the handrails and in the beautiful stained-glass windows in the staircases. These details are luxurious features and were deliberately used in low-rent workers' housing – as a reminder of the credo expressed by earlier Vienna social housing that 'housing for the poor should never look poor'. Gratte-Ciel may appear like a stage-setting for a contemporary American movie[1] but it is primarily the artistic expression of a political idea aiming at the creation of whole new communities in an industrial city. It is today a listed building complex and has undergone extensive renovation in recent years.

1 Devinaz, 2004

Die Wohnhausanlage Gratte-Ciel im Lyoner Vorort Villeurbanne gehört zu jenen Bauten, die offenbar nicht in die gängige Architekturtheorie passen und daher kaum bekannt sind. Dabei kann die Planung von Môrice Leroux in der Nachfolge von Tony Garniers Cité industrielle gesehen werden: ein Sozialwohnungsbau mit ungewöhnlich hohem Standard. Die Anlage besteht aus 1500 Wohnungen in zwei parallelen Blocks sowie dem ›Palais de travail‹ (Palast der Arbeit) mit Gewerkschaftsräumen, Arbeiterklub, Schwimmbad, Theater und der Proletarischen Universität. Den Eingang zur Wohnbebauung bilden die zwei Hochhäuser, an die sich zehngeschossige Blocks mit rückversetzten Terrassengeschossen anschließen – eine Referenz an die amerikanische Hochhausarchitektur und an Antonio Sant'Elias futuristische Stadtentwürfe, aber auch an die berühmten Projekte von Henri Sauvage in Paris. Aufwendige Art-Déco-Elemente finden sich an den Eingangstüren, Handläufen und Treppenhausfenstern. Ähnlich wie in den Wiener Gemeindebauten galt, »dass Architektur für die Armen niemals arm wirken darf«. Auch wenn die Anlage Gratte-Ciel wie eine Kulisse für zeitgenössische amerikanische Filme wirken mag, stellt sie doch vor allem den künstlerischen Ausdruck einer politischen Idee dar.

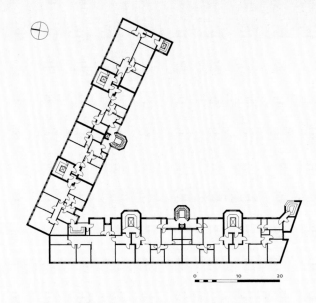

Horia Creangà ARO Building ARO-Gebäude Bucharest Bukarest Romania Rumänien 1934

As Art Deco has often been seen as the luxurious and somewhat superficial counterpart to socially-orientated, modernist building, it was usually applied to up-market, private residences rather than to multi-storey housing. In Europe, the city of Bucharest, Romania, is a remarkable exception. Having grown into a metropolis later than most cities in Europe, a number of foreign architects were invited to contribute to the rapid city development in the 1920s and '30s. At the same time, Romanian architects had maintained the contact with world-famous Romanian artists living abroad (mostly in Paris), among them Brancusi, Tzara, Enescu and Ionesco. Thus the French influence was dominant, and the Art Deco Style soon became common in Bucharest, often mixed with a 'muted' [2] modern architecture and with constructivism. Two architects are outstanding: Horia Creangà with the exceptional ARO Building (1934) which included seventy-three apartments, office and retail premises, medical practices and a large cinema, and the Swiss-trained

Marcel Iancu, a Dadaist, who built the Bazaltin Residential and Office Block (1935). Both buildings occupy prestigious locations on the grand boulevards. According to Iancu "contemporary architecture can only be anti-decorative. Its beauty resides in the play of relations and volumes … Its unity resides in geometry…, and its wisdom resides in the modesty and vigorous expression of the material." [3] The Bazaltin Building shows Iancu's extraordinarily creative play of volumes, using stepped-back storeys – as Sauvage and Leroux had done – to reconcile its massive dimensions [4] with the existing small-scale urban fabric.

Outside Europe the cities of Cape Town, Johannesburg and Miami hold a great number of outstanding Art Deco residential buildings.

2   Nerdinger, in: dos Santos, 2001, p. 3
3   Iancu, 1930, p. 10
4   dos Santos, 2001, p. 114

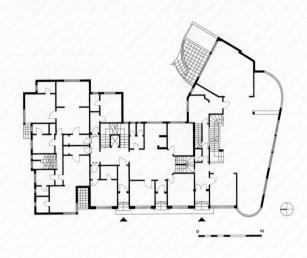

Marcel Iancu **Bazaltin Residential and Office Block** Wohn- und Geschäftshaus Bazaltin   Bucharest Bukarest   Romania Rumänien   1935

Art Déco, oft als luxuriöser und eher oberflächlicher Gegenpol zum sozial orientierten Neuen Bauen betrachtet, fand sich im allgemeinen eher im privaten Einfamilienhaus als im mehrgeschossigen Wohnungsbau. Eine bemerkenswerte Ausnahme bildete die rumänische Hauptstadt **Bukarest**, die in den 1920er-Jahren einen gewaltigen Aufschwung nahm. Da die rumänischen Künstler intensive Kontakte nach Frankreich hatten, wurde der Art-Déco-Stil, oft vermengt mit konstruktivistischen Details, rasch populär. Zu den interessantesten Wohnungsbauten gehören das **ARO-Gebäude** von **Horia Creangà** (1934) und das Wohn- und Geschäftshaus **Bazaltin** von **Marcel Iancu** (1935). Eine große Zahl außergewöhnlicher Art-Déco-Wohnbauten findet sich außerdem in **Kapstadt**, **Johannesburg** und **Miami**.

THE 1940S AND ’50S: VARIATIONS OF MODERNISM

1940ER- UND 50ER-JAHRE: VARIANTEN DER MODERNE

RECONSTRUCTION OF URBANITY   REKONSTRUKTION DER URBANITÄT

Auguste Perret
Place de l'Hôtel de Ville
Le Havre   France Frankreich   1947–1954

The reconstruction of the City of Le Havre, which had almost completely been destroyed during WW II, was seen as a task of national importance; this is why already in 1944 the Ministry for Construction and Urban Planning commissioned one of the most famous French architects with plans for a whole new inner city: Auguste Perret. Construction started in 1947 and was completed in 1954, the year Perret died. In the case of Le Havre, the term reconstruction visibly takes on a double meaning: the physical re-building of a national symbol and the re-creation of traditional (and typically French) urban forms. Thus, the master plan is based on the usual concept of streets with uniform building heights, interrupted by large squares and by symmetrically placed higher blocks – in the tradition of Beaux Arts planning rather than in the modernist CIAM approach. This concept is further underlined by the classical composition of the Haussmann-style façades, the buildings encircling semi-closed courtyards (*ilots*). Consequently Perret's masterplan has been char-acterized as old-fashioned and academic[1] compared to Le Corbusier's 'unités d'habitation' of the same period.

But this emphasis on Perret's classicism hides the innovative aspects. For the first time ever the state pre-financed housing by 100 per cent, making high-standard dwellings affordable for the working class population and, to reduce construction costs, standardization was introduced on a level unknown in any previous housing programme. Following his credo of 'Normalisation, d'abord' (first, normalization) Perret developed a construction system based on a 0.52-metre module. This resulted in a planning grid of 6.52 metres to be respected by the architects of all new buildings, and to the pre-fabrication of most building parts. Perret exposed the skeleton of the buildings which he declared a principle of classicism, and he favoured concrete which he found 'more noble than stone'. His humanist approach to large-scale planning is also reflected by other details; for example, windows are vertical (in fact the traditional French

porte-fenêtre) as 'horizontality expresses death, verticality is the true human frame',[2] and the kitchen was integrated into the living area (*séjour*) to create a room for the whole family. At the same time, these kitchens – also called 'grill rooms' – were highly standardized.

The quality of construction is extraordinary, Perret giving detailed instructions to the other architects while supervising much of the work himself. He also insisted on integrating landscape planning. This can best be seen at the huge Place de l'Hôtel de Ville where public buildings and (social) housing estates surround a thoroughly designed open space with fountains and trees. The plan for Le Havre thus proved that standardization and pre-fabrication would not automatically result in monotony, and that large-scale planning need not automatically become inhuman. It also provided possibilities for very different architectural styles: When the dynamic Communist city council invited Oscar Niemeyer to design a new cultural centre – the 'Volcano' to be completed in 1976 – one of the most exciting urban spaces in contemporary European city planning was created.

1   for example by Benevolo, vol. 2, 1978, pp. 402–05
2   see: Techniques et Architecture, nos. 7–8, 1948, and
    nos. 5–6, 1951

Mit dem Wiederaufbau der im Zweiten Weltkrieg fast völlig zerstörten Stadt Le Havre wurde Auguste Perret bereits im Jahr 1944 beauftragt. Die Bauarbeiten begannen 1947 und dauerten bis 1954. Der Begriff Rekonstruktion bekam hier eine doppelte Bedeutung: als physische Wiedererrichtung eines nationalen Symbols, aber auch als Wiedererschaffung einer traditionellen (französischen) Urbanität. Perrets Masterplan nahm daher die traditionelle Abfolge von Straßenfronten mit einheitlicher Bauhöhe und Plätzen mit symmetrisch angeordneten höheren Gebäuden auf, mit klassischen Haussmann-Fassaden und halböffentlichen Innenhöfen. Daher wurde die Planung im Vergleich zu Le Corbusiers gleichzeitig geplanten Unités d'Habitation als überholt und akademisch kritisiert.

Die Betonung von Perrets Klassizismus verdeckt aber die innovativen Aspekte: die erstmalig komplett staatliche Finanzierung von Sozialwohnungen sowie den hohen Grad an Standardisierung. Perret entwickelte ein Modulsystem, das die Vorfertigung fast aller Bauteile ermöglichte. Das tragende Skelett blieb sichtbar, denn Perret fand Beton »edler als Stein«. Seine humanistische Einstellung zeigte sich in zahlreichen Details wie der Integration der Küche in den großen Wohnraum. Le Havre beweist, dass Standardisierung nicht automatisch monoton sein, dass Planung im großen Maßstab nicht unmenschlich werden muss.

Mario Ridolfi, Ludovico Quaroni **Tiburtino** **Rome Rom** **Italy Italien** 1950

City planning in post-WW II Europe was confronted with a number of difficulties, including the lack of financing and materials, the brain-drain produced by expulsion and emigration and, not least, a cultural shock, notably in post-fascist countries. While in France it seemed logical to continue pre-war classicism, this was virtually impossible in Italy where classicist planning was now associated with Mussolini's gigantism. Thus, young architects looking for a new artistic expression found it in the arts rather than in architecture. The concept of 'neorealismo' cinema which dealt with the daily reality of ordinary people was applied to new housing estates, with surprising success. Using vernacular, uneven – or 'organic'– forms, such estates aimed at creating traditional Italian urban environments. Probably the best example is the large Tiburtino area for 'INA-casa' social housing in Rome. The masterplan (1950) is by Mario Ridolfi and Ludovico Quaroni, while several architects participated in the planning of the housing estate with some 800 dwellings. The architectural repertoire reaches from three-level terraced housing to eight-storey blocks, with houses stepped back and forth, public and semi-public spaces, pedestrian zones, passages, gardens, balconies, pergolas, integrated shops and ateliers, and varied roof forms … What could be rather chaotic follows an underlying common understanding of urban space and of its functions in a democratic and diversified society. Tiburtino, like traditional Italian towns, offers options rather than solutions.

Ignazio Gardella   Zattere Co-op   Venice Venedig   Italy Italien   1954–1958

This neorealist design approach was taken up by many other Italian cities. A small but very charming project can be found in Venice – definitely not an easy place to fit in modern architecture. The Zattere Co-op (1954–58) housing was designed by Ignazio Gardella, a prominent representative of pre-war 'rationalism'. Although higher than its neighbours the building preserves the balance between the prevailing gothic style and the necessities of a modern apartment complex.

In Italien griff man nach dem Klassizismus der Mussolini-Ära bewusst auf traditionelle Bauformen zurück und orientierte sich dabei am volkstümlichen Neorealismus des italienischen Films. Zu den besten Beispielen gehören die Sozialwohnungsbauten der Siedlung Tiburtino in Rom, aufbauend auf dem Masterplan von Mario Ridolfi und Ludovico Quaroni (1950), sowie das viel kleinere Genossenschaftshaus Zattere Co-op in Venedig von Ignazio Gardella (1954–1958).

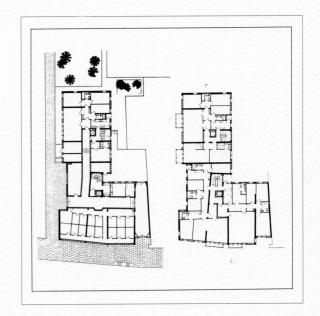

THE HOUSING MACHINE DIE WOHNMASCHINE

Le Corbusier
Unité d'Habitation
Marseilles Marseille   France Frankreich   1947–1952

The huge apartment block which Le Corbusier designed for the Boulevard Michelet in a Marseilles suburb is now regarded as one of the icons of 20th-century architecture. The idea developed gradually, following the architect's intensive studies of the relationship between the intimacy of private living space and the planning of large urban settlements. Le Corbusier had first addressed this problem in his 'Immeubles Villas' project of 1922 and, during WW II, worked on theoretical solutions for post-war reconstruction, including refugee housing, the Modulor – his famous theory on human-scale proportion – and his *brises-soleil*. In 1944 Le Corbusier proposed a low-cost housing programme of pre-fabricated, two-storey 'unités d'habitation transitoires' (temporary housing units), with rows of two-level apartments divided by a corridor. This was later developed into higher building blocks resulting in the 'unité d'habitation de grandeur conforme' with some 400 dwellings, shops, kindergarten, laundry, car park and leisure facilities. Finally, the Ministry for Urban Planning and Reconstruction commissioned Le Corbusier with the first 'unité' to be built in Marseilles.

The concept of the 'unité d'habitation' is based on a number of assumptions. First, it aims at comfortable, yet affordable urban living on a broad scale, which requires standardization for mass production; secondly, it expresses the idea of the *cité-jardin verticale* (vertical garden city) with high-rise housing in an open landscape; thirdly, it is a functionalist housing block with an expansive integrated infrastructure; fourthly, all dimensions are based on the 'Modulor' scheme. It is Le Corbusier's architecture, however, which makes the building truly unique. Apart from the already known 'typically Corbu' elements – pilotis, *brises-soleil* – it is characterized by the masterly crafted concrete building parts which culminate in the stunning plasticity of the roof terrace. A continuous play of light and shadows is created by the balcony niches, painted in bright red, blue, yellow and green. Pevsner admired it as a 'liberation from the dictatorship of cubes'[1].

The apartments are two-storeyed allowing orientation to two sides, and L-shaped in the cross-section making corridors necessary only on every third level. This scheme closely resem-

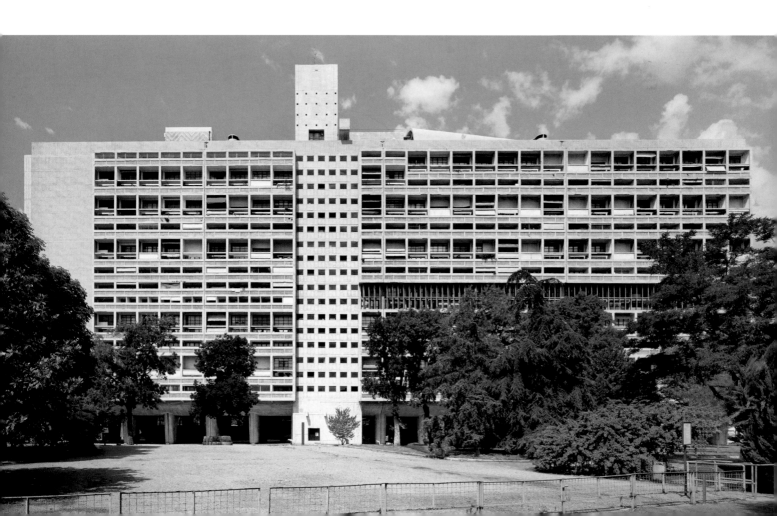

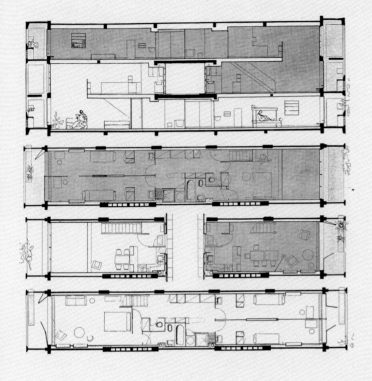

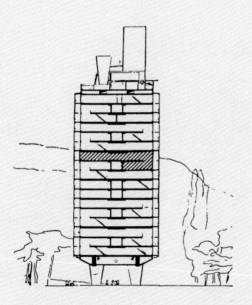

bles the projects of collective housing which had been developed in the 1920s by Soviet architects. Although rather narrow and low, the flats seem spacious due to the double height living rooms. Shops, cafeteria, post-office, etc. are situated along the internal 'street' on the seventh and eighth floor, which can also be recognized by the different façade elements. The roof terrace on the eighteenth floor provides space for a swimming pool, a playground, a bar and a running track.

Although the 'unité' has been criticized because of the narrowness of the flats, the monotony of the corridors and the failure of the internal 'urban' infrastructure – shops were inaccessible to non-residents and therefore unprofitable – it remains an impressive example of a revolutionary new approach to city planning and to collective housing. As such, it stands in the French tradition of Charles Fourier and Saint-Simon. And it remains, of course, the expression of a personal belief: that its programmatic utilitarianism need not hamper artistic freedom, and that a 'machine' – at least from a housing point of view – could provide the prerequisites for contemporary yet individual urban living.

1 Pevsner, 1968, p. 415

Der große Wohnblock in Marseille ist eine Ikone der Architektur des 20. Jahrhunderts. Le Corbusier hatte das Konzept schrittweise entwickelt, beginnend 1922 mit den Immeubles Villas und zahlreichen theoretischen Überlegungen wie dem Modulor-Maßsystem. Der Plan einer ›unité d'habitation de grandeur conforme‹ mit rund 400 Wohnungen beruhte auf einer Reihe von Annahmen: Errichtung komfortabler, erschwinglicher Wohnungen durch Standardisierung im großen Maßstab, Realisierung der ›cité-jardin verticale‹ (vertikale Gartenstadt) durch Hochhäuser in einer offenen Landschaft, Integration der Infrastruktur in das Gebäude als funktionalistische Wohnmaschine und Entwicklung aller Maße aus dem vom menschlichen Körper abgeleiteten Modulor. Vor allem aber ist das Gebäude durch Le Corbusiers Architektur geprägt, durch seinen meisterhaften Umgang mit Sichtbeton,

besonders in der plastischen Formgebung der Dachaufbauten, die Pilotis, die ›brises-soleil‹ und die farbigen Balkonnischen mit ihrem Spiel von Licht und Schatten. Die Wohnungen sind zweigeschossig und im Schnitt L-förmig, wodurch nur auf jeder dritten Etage ein Gang benötigt wird – eine deutliche Anlehnung an die früheren sowjetischen Kollektivhäuser. Einkaufsmöglichkeiten befinden sich an der internen ›Straße‹ im siebten und achten Stock.

Trotz mancher Mängel wurde die Unité d'Habitation zum Ausdruck einer revolutionär neuen städteplanerischen Auffassung und eines persönlichen Glaubens: dass Funktionalismus nicht im Gegensatz zu künstlerischer Freiheit stehen muss, und dass die ›Maschine‹ die Voraussetzungen für zeitgemäßes individuelles Wohnen schaffen kann.

Alvar Aalto   Hansaviertel   Berlin   Germany Deutschland   1957

Le Corbusier   Hansaviertel   Berlin   Germany Deutschland   1957

The list of architects to participate in the Berlin exhibition reads like a 'Who-is-Who in Architecture' and includes such names as Walter Gropius, Oscar Niemeyer, Arne Jacobsen, Johannes H. van den Broek and Jacob B. Bakema, Alvar Aalto and Wassili Luckhardt. On the other hand, its overall urban planning seems un-ambitious and does not reach the spatial qualities of the British or Scandinavian housing areas being designed at that time. This may explain why the Hansaviertel has never become a point of reference for world architecture. Nevertheless, some of the housing schemes are excellent, as shown by the Alvar Aalto project.

Aalto aimed at combining the advantages of urban living with those of a free-standing house.[3] He grouped the rooms around large private atriums, providing each apartment with an open space protected from the outside. On the ground floor the spacious entrance hall serves as a communication area for all residents; glazing is generous and the slight shift in axes results in a slightly curved structure which reflects the moderate modernist architecture found in Scandinavia in the 1950s rather than the austere pre-war Neues Bauen. This was a strong antithesis to any kind of 'housing machine'. If not by its city planning qualities, new housing concepts could profit from the Berlin exhibition by the innovative solutions found for flexible and open floor plans.

2   C.f. eg. Boesiger, vol. 8, 1970
3   Nerdinger, 2000, p. 34

Following Marseilles, Le Corbusier was invited to plan several 'unités' for other French cities, including Nanterre, Meaux, Briey-en-Foret and Firminy-Vert. At Firminy he also designed a youth centre, a stadium and a civic centre, making it his most important urban ensemble in Europe.[2] Finally, the architect participated in the 1957 Interbau-Exhibition in the Hansaviertel in Berlin. Here, the 'Modulor' scheme gave way to more generous proportions of flats, but the building quality lacked by far the technical mastership of the first 'unités'.

Le Corbusier errichtete weitere Unités in Frankreich und im Rahmen der Interbau 1957 im Berliner Hansaviertel. Dieses wurde unter Mitwirkung zahlreicher prominenter Architekten geplant, zeichnet sich aber weniger durch besondere städtebauliche Qualität aus als durch innovative Lösungen für flexible Wohnungsgrundrisse. Zu den besten Arbeiten gehört der Wohnblock von Alvar Aalto, der die Wohnräume um großzügige private Atrien gruppiert – zugleich eine Antithese zu jeder Art von ›Wohnmaschine‹.

STEEL CLASSICISM KLASSIZISMUS IN STAHL

Ludwig Mies van der Rohe
Lake Shore Drive Apartments
Chicago   Illinois, USA   1948–1951

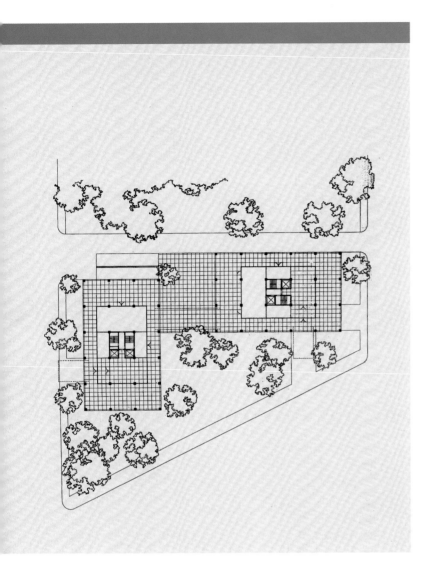

The course of the American architectural development "was changed drastically by the European architects who came to the United States in the late '30s. Without them one suspects American architecture might have tried to remain eclectic..."[1] This was especially true for the German immigrants. "Americans, whose ultra-refined desire to polish"[2] tended to result in their rejection of Le Corbusier's sculptural freedom, more easily accepted modernist architects like Walter Gropius, Marcel Breuer and – most of all – Ludwig Mies van der Rohe. One of the reasons for this was that Mies had already occupied himself with skyscraper design in the 1920s, studying the possibilities of steel-and-glass constructions and their effects on the architectural form. Thus he was ready to alter drastically what was regarded as the ultimate American building type.

Mies, appointed Head of the Architecture Department of the Illinois Institute of Technology in 1938, had just finished the groundbreaking IIT Campus on Chicago's South Side when he was commissioned to design two high-rise apartment blocks at the prestigious Lake Shore Drive location. Although functionalist at a first glance, the elegant, up-market estate was a radical departure from functional expression. Both towers are steel skeletons embedded in concrete – for safety reasons, but the concrete is not left exposed on the exterior. Instead, black steel beams are applied to the façades, simulating a mere steel construction. All flats had the same grey curtains, thus disguising the variety of interiors. And the fenestrian pattern – with the outer windows in each group of four being slightly narrower – is emphasized by vertical steel I-beams which serve no practical function.

This classical approach is not surprising. According to Mies, it was not light and shade that mattered in architecture any more but the play of reflections on the glass wall. As in the 1929 Barcelona Pavilion, the delicacy of the steel members "proved that monumentality was accessible by means not of column shams but of splendid materials and a noble spatial rhythm."[3] In other words, monumentality was still the aim and style was not simply an expression of function. In spite of his repetitive façades that were often misunderstood, Mies' architecture was rooted more in 'romantic classicism'[4] than in pre-war modernism. Classicism is achieved by the elaborate use of a single element – the glass wall – with its rhythmical repetition, the principle of the Greek temple. 'Romanticism' on the other hand, is expressed by the intelligent response to the beautiful location and the open space beneath the buildings which allow an unrestricted view of the lake.

However, the most intriguing new aspect of the Lake Shore Drive Apartments lies in the brilliant use of materials, a quality virtually never achieved before in any housing scheme and only to be surpassed by Mies' own Seagram Building in New York of 1957. Both firmly established modern design as an American national style: 'America had finally achieved an architecture compatible with her industrial might.'[5]

1 Burchard, Bush-Brown, 1966, p. 354
2 Ibid., 1966, p. 362
3 Pevsner, 1968, p. 416
4 Jacobus, 1966, p. 60
5 Pevsner, 1968, p. 405

Die amerikanische Architektur wurde durch die Immigration europäischer – vor allem deutscher – Architekten aus ihrem Eklektizismus befreit. Besonders Mies van der Rohe, der sich schon in den 1920er-Jahren theoretisch mit Wolkenkratzern aus Stahl und Glas befasst hatte, trug zur radikalen Neuinterpretation dieses ›amerikanischen‹ Bautyps bei. Nach Vollendung der bahnbrechenden Neubauten für das Illinois Institute of Technology (IIT) in Chicago entwarf er mit den Lake Shore Drive Apartments elegante Luxuswohnungen in bester Lage. Trotz der klaren Architektursprache vollzog er hier eine radikale Abkehr vom Funktionalismus: Die Betonummantelung der Stahlskelette wird durch außen aufgebrachte I-Träger kaschiert, einheitlich graue Vorhänge verstecken die unterschiedlichen Interieurs und der Fensterraster wird durch vertikale, funktionslose Stahlelemente betont. Wie im Barcelona Pavillon von 1929 setzte Mies bei den Lake Shore Drive Apartments auf eine Monumentalität, die nicht durch Säulenordnungen, sondern durch Material und Rhythmus erzeugt wird. Stil ist nicht ausschließlich ein Ausdruck von Funktion. Mies folgte eher einem »romantischen Klassizismus« als der Vorkriegsmoderne – klassisch, weil die Wiederholung gleichartiger Elemente dem Prinzip des griechischen Tempels entspricht, romantisch in der sensiblen Reaktion auf die Schönheit der Lage am See. Vor allem aber besticht die zuvor niemals erreichte Präzision der Materialverwendung. Wie durch Mies' Seagram Building in New York von 1957 wurde damit die Moderne zum amerikanischen Nationalstil erhoben.

Ludwig Mies van der Rohe   Promontory Apartments   Chicago, Illinois   USA   1946

Drawing of preliminary steel design Zeichnung des Entwurfs aus Stahl

The success of the Lake Shore Drive Apartments let architectural theory somehow miss another extraordinary housing estate by Mies: the 1946 Promontory Apartments in Chicago. Built on the shore of Lake Michigan like their famous successors they show a surprisingly different, yet typically Miesian, treatment of a high-rise residential scheme. Mies developed a strict grid of rectangular coordinates on which he experimented with alternative construction systems: steel and glass, or reinforced concrete with brick fillings. Finally, the concrete and brick version was chosen, the frame being emphasized by the projection of the columns. This gives the huge block a stronger perspective and underlines the continuity of the wall. Because of the greater load on the lower parts the columns are stepped back at the sixth, eleventh and sixteenth storeys. Mies deliberately applied a tectonic order developed by the 19th-century Chicago School, replacing the differentiation in the height of the façades by a rhythmical repetition of identical elements. At the same time this made it possible to maintain the human scale – which defines the repetitive elements, not the composition as a whole – regardless of the size of the building. The Promontory Apartments form an impressive, almost timeless, artistic statement on the shores of Lake Michigan.

Bei den bereits 1946 errichteten **Promontory Apartments** in Chicago entschied man sich für ein Stahlbetonskelett mit Ziegelausfachung auf einem strengen Raster. Mies griff hier bewusst auf die Tektonik der Chicagoer Schule des 19. Jahrhunderts zurück, indem er die klassische Fassadenordnung durch eine rhythmische Wiederholung gleichartiger, am menschlichen Maßstab orientierter Elemente ersetzte – ein eindrucksvolles, fast zeitloses künstlerisches Statement am Ufer des Michigansees.

SOUTHERN MODERNISM MODERNISMUS IM SÜDEN

Affonso Edoardo Reidy
Pedregulho Housing Complex Wohnblock Pedregulho
Rio de Janeiro Brazil Brasilien 1950–1952

Few housing estates have ever been received with such enthusiasm as the Pedregulho Complex in Rio de Janeiro. Among its admirers were the Swiss architect Max Bill – who would have liked to have lived there[1] – and Walter Gropius.[2] In 1953, it won the gold medal at the first international Bienal de São Paulo. What was it that made architects like Siegfried Giedion say that it should be seen as an example for every other city?

When Affonso Edoardo Reidy, who had previously worked with Le Corbusier, Lucio Costa and Oscar Niemeyer, designed the Pedregulho Estate, he was contributing towards the effort made by Brazil's post-war leftist government to solve the social problems in the big cities. Housing and health were the most urgent issues. According to the plans of the Rio Popular Housing Department, Pedregulho – a suburban area of some 50,000 square metres – was to become a model estate for low-income council workers. It includes three residential blocks (a fourth one was not completed), a school, a sports centre, a health centre, a laundry, a market, playgrounds and a kindergarten. Among the housing units, the 260-metre serpentine building, with some 270 apartments, which adheres closely to the existing topography, became the symbol of the new development – and, in fact, a symbol of Brazil's social housing policy. While its curved form is reminiscent of Le Corbusier's plans for Algier, it is also a daring example of post-war Brazilian architecture. It has been described as one of the most fabulous expressions of internationalism while, at the same time, revolting against it.[3] The six-storey block stands on pilotis with the entrance level on the third floor. Access from the hilltop is accentuated by an impressive void, making the enormous mass of the building seemingly float above the city.

It was, however, the combination of social housing, architectural quality and the hygiene programme which made this housing scheme really unique. Regular health checks and frequent inspections of the apartments were obligatory, each household receiving free detergents along the lines that 'the inhabitants had to remain clean'.[4] Pedregulho was to become the physical expression of Brazil's social reform. Sadly, it became the opposite. With a declining economy and the defeat of democracy the model estate fell to vandalism and crime.[5] It shared the fate of many other reformatory housing projects: that the social problems could not be solved by a single estate and even less by architecture alone. The social experiment may have failed but, powerful in its appearance alone, Pedregulho survived as 'a timeless monument to an untimely society'.[6]

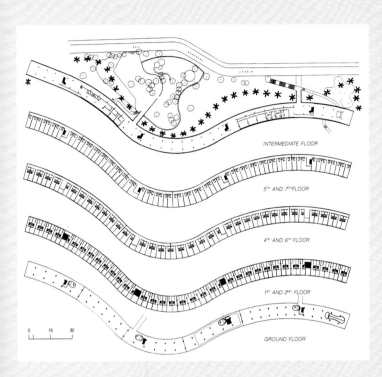

INTERMEDIATE FLOOR

5TH AND 7TH FLOOR

4TH AND 6TH FLOOR

1ST AND 2ND FLOOR

GROUND FLOOR

0 15 30

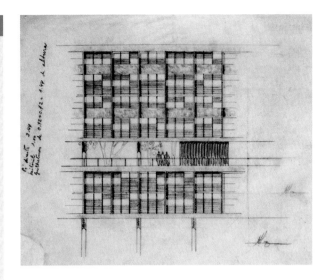

1 Bill, 1954, pp. 238, 239
2 Gropius, 1954, pp. 236, 237
3 C.f. e.g. Pevsner, 1968, pp. 427–31
4 Weiss, Fischer, 2002
5 Pedregulho even served as the background for the film 'Central Station'
   which deals with Brazil's corrupt policies and crime against children
6 Weiss, Fischer, 2002

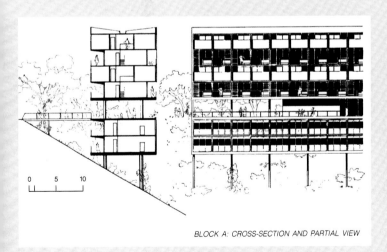

0 5 10

BLOCK A: CROSS-SECTION AND PARTIAL VIEW

Wenige Wohnungsbauten wurden mit soviel Enthusiasmus be-
grüßt wie der Pedregulho-Komplex von Affonso Edoardo Reidy in
Rio de Janeiro. 1953 gewann er die Goldmedaille der 1. Internationalen Biennale von São Paulo, zu seinen Bewunderern gehörten
Walter Gropius, Max Bill und Siegfried Giedion. Die Musteranlage
für städtische Angestellte mit niedrigem Einkommen, bestehend
aus drei Wohnblöcken, Schule, Kindergarten, Sportanlagen, Ge-
sundheitszentrum, Wäscherei und einem Markt, war Teil des Sozi-
alprogramms der linken Nachkriegsregierungen Brasiliens. Der
schlangenförmige Wohnblock, der den Hügel dominiert, wurde
damit nicht nur zu einem Symbol des peripheren Stadtviertels,
sondern der brasilianischen Sozialwohnungspolitik insgesamt.
Der riesige Bau auf Pilotis scheint über der Stadt zu schweben.
Seine gekurvte Form erinnert an Le Corbusiers Planung für Algier,
stellt aber auch eines der überzeugendsten Beispiele der brasilianischen Nachkriegsarchitektur dar, das als Ausdruck des Inter-
nationalismus und zugleich als Revolte gegen ihn beschrieben
wurde.

Wirklich einzigartig wurde Pedregulho aber durch die Verbindung von Wohnungs- und Gesundheitsprogramm. Die Mieter
mussten sich zu regelmäßigen Untersuchungen und Inspektionen
der Wohnungen verpflichten, jeder Haushalt erhielt kostenlos
Waschmittel. Pedregulho sollte sichtbarer Ausdruck der brasilianischen Sozialreform sein. Doch das Gegenteil trat ein: Infolge
der wirtschaftlichen Schwierigkeiten und der Niederwerfung der
Demokratie wurde die Anlage zu einem Zentrum des Vandalismus
und der Kriminalität. Wieder einmal zeigte sich, dass gesellschaftliche Probleme nicht allein durch Architektur lösbar sind.

Lucio Costa Super Quadras Brasilia Brasil Brasilien 1956–1960

The same reformatory spirit characterized Brazil's most ambitious project, the construction of a whole new capital city by the architects Lucio Costa and Oscar Niemeyer. Following the intention of President J. Kubitschek, Brasilia should present an entirely new model of city planning based on the ideals of democracy and welfare. Apart from the well-known, sometimes rather pathetic public buildings, the architects designed a model housing complex which is reminiscent of Le Corbusier's 'Immeubles Villas': the Super Quadra. Several freestanding housing units on pilotis, almost identical in length and height (six storeys), occupy large rectangular plots and share a precisely defined, common infrastructure. This was based on the assumption that land was public and would only be sold after the planning of the housing estates. Again, as in the case of Pedregulho, though on a much bigger scale, Brasilia suffered under the economic and political developments within the country. By and by, Costa's and Niemeyer's ideal city was surrounded by drab middle-class areas and *favelas* – although, ironically, this helped to make it a more lively city.

Vom gleichen reformerischen Anspruch war die Gründung der neuen Hauptstadt Brasilia gekennzeichnet. Sie sollte zum völlig neuen Stadtmodell des demokratischen Wohlfahrtsstaats werden. Lucio Costa und Oscar Niemeyer, deren öffentliche Bauten weltberühmt wurden, sahen für die Wohnviertel große rechteckige Grundstücke vor, auf denen die Super Quadras, einheitliche Wohnblöcke auf Pilotis, gemeinsam mit einer genau definierten Infrastruktur errichtet werden sollten. Bauland sollte in öffentlicher Hand bleiben und erst nach der Planung der Wohnhausanlagen verkauft werden. Wie Pedregulho litt auch das ehrgeizige Projekt Brasilia unter der wirtschaftlichen und politischen Entwicklung Brasiliens: Nach und nach umgaben öde Mittelklassegebiete und Favelas die Idealstadt von Costa und Niemeyer – was aber ironischerweise auch zur Entstehung einer lebendigen Stadt beitrug.

Mario Romañach   Evangelina Aristigueta de Vidaña Residence   Havana Havanna   Cuba Kuba   1956

Unlike the architecture of Brazil or Mexico the history of Modernism in Cuba has never received much international recognition, although the city of Havana holds a staggering number of 1940s and 1950s buildings of outstanding quality.[7] In many projects, traditional elements like patios and galleries were combined with the bare surfaces of the International Style. Among the most influential architects were Mario Romañach who designed the Evangelina Aristigueta de Vidaña Residence (1956), and Max Borges Recio with the Ildefonso Semeillán Apartments (1954). Recio had already gained recognition for the extraordinary structure of the Nautical Club and also became known for his José Martí Stadium, both buildings adapting the modernist syntax to an individual Caribbean language. But it was the Cuban housing estates where the Southern International Style found its most exuberant expression.

Im Gegensatz zur Architektur in Brasilien oder Mexiko ist die Moderne Kubas wenig bekannt. Dabei gibt es allein in Havanna rund 200 Gebäude des Modernismus, der oft durch lokale Elemente wie Patios und Balkone ergänzt wurde. Zu den einflussreichsten Architekten gehören Mario Romañach mit dem Wohnhaus Evangelina Aristigueta de Vidaña (1956) in Havana und Max Borges Recio mit den Ildefonsa Semeillán Apartments (1954). In den kubanischen Wohnhausanlagen fand der Internationale Stil des Südens seinen überschwänglichsten Ausdruck.

There is a similarly fresh and open interpretaton of the modernist style in the city of Casablanca, Morocco, where – mostly European – architects intended to adapt it to the hot climate. One of the best examples is the 1953 Sidi Othman housing estate by the Swiss architects André Studer and Jean Hentsch who combined the flat façades of the International Style with the sculptural qualities of local vernacular building.[8] The six-storey block dissolves into a pattern of box-like elements supported by columns. One of the aims is, of course, to provide the two-bedroom apartments with shade; but the building is also a stunning predecessor of another icon of 20th-century housing architecture, the 1967 'Habitat' in Montreal.

7   Rodriguez, 2000, lists more than 200 modernist buildings in Havana
8   Cohen, Eleb, 2002

Eine ähnlich unvoreingenommene Aneignung des modernistischen Stils findet sich in der marokkanischen Stadt Casablanca, wo unter anderen Europäern die Schweizer Architekten André Studer und Jean Hentsch die große Wohnanlage Sidi Othman (1953) planten. Der sechsstöckige Block ist in ein abstraktes Muster schachtelartiger Räume aufgelöst, die auf schlanken Säulen ruhen und Schatten bieten. Das Gebäude ist zugleich ein verblüffender Vorläufer des Habitat-Projektes in Montreal (1967), einer Ikone der Architektur des 20. Jahrhunderts.

NEW TOWNS AND SATELLITE CITIES
NEUE STÄDTE UND TRABANTENSTÄDTE

Hubert Bennett
Alton Estate
Roehampton, London   **Great Britain Großbritannien**   **1955–1959**

With WW II still raging British architects and city planners started to discuss reconstruction strategies. In 1942, MARS – the British affiliate of CIAM – presented a model for London, splitting up the densely built-up city into different areas, separated by green zones. Two years later the London County Council adopted a plan which foresaw the re-housing of some 400,000 inner-city residents to areas outside the green belt. These plans were taken up by the groundbreaking New Towns Act in 1946. While, in accordance with the 1936 Housing Act, state subsidies remained unchanged, a whole new structure was established on the administrational level, including Development Corporations for each of a total of seven New Towns, and Joint Planning Boards formed by different County Councils. The British approach was unique in Europe and therefore attracted the close attention of city planners world-wide.

New town planning, however, did not automatically mean modern architecture. Most housing projects were characterized by national vernacular rather than by pre-war modernism. It was Alton Estate in Roehampton, bordering Richmond Park, which finally allowed a breakthrough of modernist architecture. Planned in 1958 to 1959 to house nearly 10,000 it consists of two large estates – Alton East and Alton West – with a mix of high-rise and low-rise housing, and with point blocks set amongst lush greenery. The architects of Alton West – notably Hubert Bennett – also adopted the Le Corbusier model of large housing units. Its concrete architecture of 'New Brutalism' was to become a symbol of the successes as well as the failures of British social housing schemes.

According to Raynar Banham, Brutalism focuses on 'the truth of materials' which makes 'the whole concept of the building plain and comprehensible. No mystery, no romanticism, no obscurities about function and circulation'.[1] Brutalist exteriors became, however, also targets for critics, arguing that the expression of architectural ideas should not come before the needs of the users. On the other hand, the natural environment was carefully integrated into the housing scheme, based on the new concept of 'townscaping'.[2]

Even if Roehampton could not escape the problems caused by the breakdown of society and vandalism which hit British social housing areas in the 1980s, it was praised as 'aesthetically the best housing estate to date',[3] and it remains one of the best-managed council housing schemes in London. It is still an impressive example for the creation of entirely new communities brought about by a government act, based on the inherent philosophy of establishing social coherence through good architecture.

1   Gallagher, 2005
2   Benevolo, vol. 2, 1978, p. 372
3   Pevsner, 1968, p. 433

Aerial view of Alton East
Luftaufnahme von Alton East

Aerial view of Alton West   Luftaufnahme von Alton West

Bereits während des Zweiten Weltkriegs hatte MARS, der britische Zweig der CIAM, Wiederaufbaupläne für London präsentiert, die auf den Bau neuer Städte außerhalb des Grüngürtels zielten. Im bahnbrechenden New Towns Act von 1946 wurden diese Pläne konkretisiert. Doch erst die Siedlung Alton Estate in Roehampton, die ab 1958 für rund 10 000 Bewohner errichtet wurde, brachte auch architektonisch den Durchbruch. Sie vereinigte unterschiedliche Bauformen, von Reihenhäusern bis zu hohen Punkthäusern, wobei Hubert Bennett auch Le Corbusiers Modell der großen ›Wohneinheiten‹ aufnahm. Seine Architektur des neuen Brutalismus wurde zum Symbol des britischen Sozialwohnungsprogramms – im Positiven wie im Negativen. Kritiker meinten, sie stelle die architektonische Idee über die Bedürfnisse ihrer Nutzer. Andererseits wurden die Bauten sorgfältig in die natürliche Umgebung eingebettet. Roehampton konnte zwar dem gesellschaftlichen Zusammenbruch der 1980er-Jahre nicht völlig entgehen, gehört aber immer noch zu den am besten verwalteten kommunalen Wohnungsbauten in London.

Sven Backström, Leif Reinius Vällingby Sweden Schweden 1952–1956

In Sweden, the cramped living conditions in urban areas led the ruling Social Democrats to strengthen the role of the state and the municipalities with regard to the provision of housing. Dwellings alone, however, were not enough. They should be integrated into complete urban environments,[4] orientated on the British New Town concept. This decentralization strategy depended on efficient public transport systems. Community centres – a common concept in Swedish urban planning – which included schools, social centres, offices, shops and cultural premises, with a direct connection to the subway network, were created to service some 6,000 residents each. At larger developments an additional 'work-housing-centre'[5] serves as a kind of new city core. The first – and most popular – of these Swedish satellite cities was to become Vällingby (chief architect Sven Markelius, 1952–56) in western Stockholm, later followed by Farsta south of the city.

Vällingby became the physical expression of a political idea: that the 'Swedish model' should be based on public power rather than on a liberal-market economy. Indeed, the degree of public intervention – the public ownership of land, public transport, a collective infrastructure, public housing connected to spatial planning concepts, etc., – was unrivalled by any other development in Western Europe. The new town was to be the very opposite of the speculative old city centres, with an emphasis on freestanding residential blocks of varying heights while preserving the natural environment. This concept is best expressed in the tower blocks by the architects Sven Backström and Leif Reinius. For the

first time landscaping was given special attention (architect Eric Glemme). The standard and quality of the housing were generally high, profiting from the remarkable state housing research programme as well as from generous state subsidies. All flats had built-in kitchens, complete bathrooms and integrated waste-disposal chutes. Social segregation was – and is – very low. Thus, Vällingby, though more urban in character than most English New Towns, has remained a convincing example of planning on a human scale. "Never before had Sweden been so modern as during the 1950s and Vällingby was the most modern of all."[6]

In Schweden führten die beengten Wohnverhältnisse in den Städten zu einer Stärkung der Rolle des Staates und der Kommunen durch die regierenden Sozialdemokraten. Dem britischen New-Town-Konzept folgend, sollten die dezentralen, an leistungsfähige öffentliche Verkehrsmittel angeschlossenen Trabantenstädte über eine komplette urbane Infrastruktur verfügen. Das von Sven Markelius geplante Vällingby (1952–1956) wurde zum sichtbaren Ausdruck des schwedischen Sozialstaatmodells mit hohem Wohnungsstandard und geringer sozialer Segregation; zugleich wurden die Wohnungsbauten – wie die markanten Punkthäuser von Sven Backström und Leif Reinius – erstmals von einer von Eric Glemme sorgfältig geplanten Landschaftsarchitektur umgeben.

Aarne Ervi, Viljo Revell   Tapiola   Espoo   Finland Finnland   1954

One of the best projects along the lines of the Vällingby planning principle is Tapiola in Espoo, Finland, developed by Aarne Ervi between 1954 and 1961. Its garden-city like setting provides high-quality living as do the strikingly modern apartment blocks by the architect Viljo Revell.[7]

In Finnland nahm Aarne Ervi das Konzept der Trabantenstadt in seinem Plan für Tapiola (1954–1961), eine Vorstadt von Espoo, auf. Die sachlich-modernen Wohnblocks wurden von Viljo Revell entworfen.

Kurt W. Leucht   Eisenhüttenstadt   Germany Deutschland   1950–1961

At the same time, the Finnish architect Alvar Aalto participated in the development of a housing area with more than 10,000 flats in Bremen, Germany. His twenty-two-storey residential tower became the hallmark of the Neue Vahr area (1956–61); its fan-shaped floor plan provides each apartment with west-facing balconies. Street-like corridors, glass partitions and an elegant vestibule contribute to the impression of spaciousness and luxury.

Meanwhile a whole new city was being constructed in East Germany – Stalinstadt, renamed Eisenhüttenstadt in 1961 – hailed as 'the first socialist city on German soil'.[8] The master plan by Kurt W. Leucht followed the Soviet model of standardized housing complexes complemented by a comprehensive infrastructure. Residential architecture ranges from vernacular classicism to 'panel construction' housing blocks. In its urban qualities and multi-functional mix, Eisenhüttenstadt was definitely more successful than most Western German satellite cities but the economic difficulties following the decline of East Germany (GDR) have turned it into a 'shrinking city' today, and large-scale demolition has been proposed. Similar new towns, among them Stalinvaros (Hungary) and Nova Huta (Poland), were built all over Eastern Europe.

Alvar Aalto war an der Planung für die Neue Vahr (1956–1961) in Bremen beteiligt; sein Hochhaus wurde zum Wahrzeichen des neuen Stadtteils. Gleichzeitig wurde in der DDR eine komplette neue Stadt errichtet: Stalinstadt, das spätere Eisenhüttenstadt (1950–1961), »die erste sozialistische Stadt auf deutschem Boden«. Der Masterplan von Kurt W. Leucht folgte dem sowjetischen Modell standardisierter Wohnungskomplexe mit genau definierter Infrastruktur. Die Architektur bewegte sich zwischen Klassizismus und Plattenbauweise, doch war Eisenhüttenstadt in seiner Multifunktionalität erfolgreicher als so manche westdeutsche Satellitenstadt – bis sie der Zusammenbruch der DDR zur ›schrumpfenden Stadt‹ machte. Ähnliche Realisierungen erfolgten in Stalinvaros (Ungarn) und Nova Huta (Polen).

4   Lindvall, 1992, p. 228–30
5   Andersson, 1997, pp. 173–75
6   Andersson, 1997, p. 173
7   Norri, 1999, pp. 230–33
8   Nerdinger, 2000, p. 58

Alvar Aalto   Neue Vahr   Bremen   Germany Deutschland   1956–1961

THE 1960S AND '70S: SOCIAL HOUSING AND THE METACITY

1960ER- UND 70ER-JAHRE:
SOZIALER WOHNUNGSBAU UND METASTADT

SUPERSTRUCTURES METASTRUKTUREN

Moshe Safdie and Associates
Habitat '67
Montreal   Quebec, Canada Kanada   1964–1967

The Habitat Estate, one of the architectural icons of the 20th century, is the work of Moshe Safdie, an architect who was born in Haifa and influenced by the early modernist architecture in Israel. Built on the occasion of the 1967 Montreal World Exposition, Habitat was conceived as a model community constructed along the St. Lawrence River. Of the originally planned 900 units, only 158 were finally built. The structure is composed of 354 pre-fabricated modules, linked by steel cables, which combine to form a three-dimensional space of pronounced sculptural quality. Their position ensures that each unit has a degree of privacy, while providing views and 'suburban amenities in an urban location'.[1] Projections and recessions

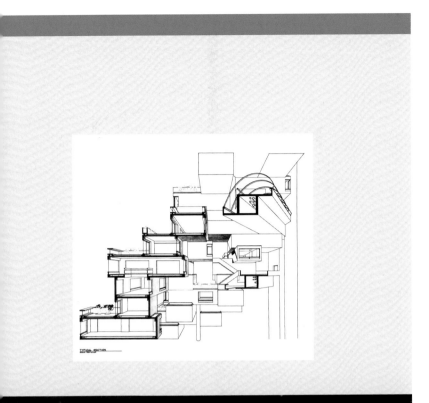

provide each apartment with a terrace on the roof of the house below.

Pedestrian streets encourage a horizontal circulation throughout the entire complex. The quality of the outdoor areas is surprising, with a great variety of private and public spaces, passage-ways, intimate corners, different access solutions and unexpected vistas. The manifold interaction of piled box-like structures and empty spaces creates a continuous change of light and shadows, while at the same time recalling a child joyfully playing with building blocks.

Habitat was planned as a prototype for a system that would streamline the building process and cut costs. Ironically, the production of the modular forms was prohibitively expensive which led to an outcry. With a few exceptions – Puerto Rico and New York – the model was not continued. Nevertheless, its influence on contemporary architecture can hardly be overestimated. Prefabrication and industrialization, as it showed clearly, need not lead to uniformity and anonymity but could create almost poetic visions of large cities based on a human scale.

1 Sharp Dennis, 1990, p. 281

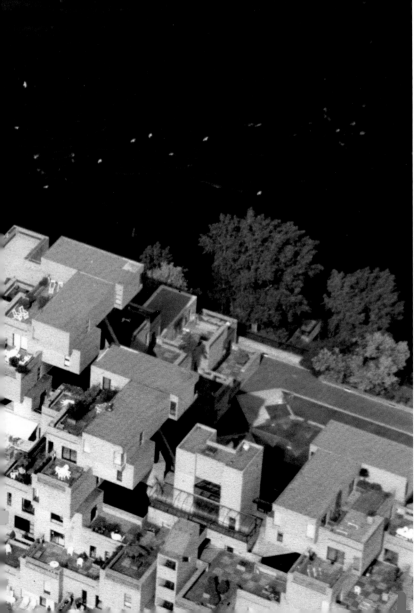

Mit der Wohnhausanlage Habitat, die Moshe Safdie 1967 anlässlich der Weltausstellung in Montreal entwarf, entstand eine der Architekturikonen des 20. Jahrhunderts. Von den geplanten 900 Wohnungen wurden allerdings nur 158 realisiert, die wie ein riesiger Baukasten aus 354 vorgefertigten Betoncontainern zusammengesetzt sind. Jeder Wohnung sollten damit Privatheit, Ausblick und »vorstädtische Qualitäten in einer städtischen Umgebung« geboten werden. Überraschend sind vor allem die vielfältigen privaten und öffentlichen Freiräume und Durchblicke, die zu einem Spiel von Licht und Schatten führen. Habitat verstand sich als Prototyp zur Vereinheitlichung der Bauproduktion und damit zur Kostenreduzierung; letztlich waren die Baukosten aber so hoch, dass es kaum zu Nachfolgeprojekten kam. Dennoch kann der Einfluss von Habitat auf die zeitgenössische Architektur kaum hoch genug eingeschätzt werden. Das Projekt zeigte deutlich, dass Vorfertigung und Industrialisierung nicht zu Uniformität und Anonymität führen müssen, sondern durchaus auch Großstädte mit menschlichem Maßstab schaffen können.

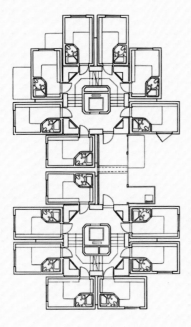

Kisho Kurokawa   Nakagin Capsule Tower   Tokyo   Japan   1970–1972

Buildings like Habitat were also part of the political and social discourse of the 1960s and early 1970s. In addition to architecture and urban design, the on-going architectural discussion encompassed the realms of sociology, political sciences, economics, philosophy and art. Flexibility, mass fabrication and open structures to serve the rapidly changing needs of a mobile society became central themes in an architect's work. The construction of new urban areas was in fact conceived as a two-step process: huge structures, supported on columns should provide 'neutral' spaces for all kinds of use – spaces for a democratic society – including dwellings to be built by residents themselves. These superstructures were often projected over imaginary locations or over whole cities, such as the famous domes by Richard Buckminster Fuller. One of the most influential architects (although he built very little himself) was Yona Friedman who formulated first ideas about flexible

housing in post-war Israel, focussing on light-weight structures in an urban context. He later worked on housing issues for UNESCO in several Third World countries.

Gebäude wie Habitat waren auch Teil und Ergebnis des politischen und gesellschaftlichen Diskurses der 1960er- und frühen 70er-Jahre, der Soziologie, Politikwissenschaften, Ökonomie, Philosophie und Kunst mit einschloss. Flexibilität, Massenproduktion und offene Strukturen für eine mobile und demokratische Gesellschaft prägten die – oft nur theoretischen – Konzepte. Yona Friedman etwa entwarf schon früh flexible Wohnbausysteme, die zu einer Trennung von Metastruktur und nutzungsneutralen Räumen führten.

Richard Dietrich, Bernd Steigerwald **Metastadt** **Wulfen** **Germany Deutschland** **1972–1976**

In Austria, the Haus-Rucker-Co group worked on transitory spaces and temporary architecture with pneumatic structures ('Mind Expander' and 'Leisuretime Explosion', 1967) while Friedrich St. Florian suggested a 'Vertical City' (1964–66). Hans Hollein designed cloud-like structures floating over Vienna (1960) and opened architecture to the pop-culture with his famous Aircraft Carrier City. In 1963 he proclaimed that 'everything is architecture'.[2] Similar projects were developed in Japan by Kisho Kurokawa (his 'Spiral City' of 1961 was followed by the famous 1972 Nakagin Capsule Tower), in France by Paul Maymont ('Ville flottante'), in Britain by Archigram ('Plug-in City')[3] and in Italy by Superstudio – with the 'Monumento continuo'[4] mocking the euphoric urban planning of the 1960s consumption-oriented society – and Archizoom ('Residential diagrams', 1970). Almost none of these projects was ever built and one of the few realized examples, the Metastadt by Richard Dietrich and Bernd Steigerwald (Wulfen, Germany, 1972–76) was demolished only ten years later due to massive technical problems. The architects' theories, however, continued to influence urban planning and housing over the following decades.

In Österreich entwickelten die Gruppe Haus-Rucker-Co und die Architekten Friedrich St. Florian und Hans Hollein ähnliche utopische Vorstellungen, in Frankreich Paul Maymont, in England Archigram und in Italien Superstudio und Archizoom. Eines der wenigen realisierten Beispiele, die Metastadt von Richard Dietrich and Bernd Steigerwald in Wulfen (1972–1976) musste bereits zehn Jahre später wegen massiver Bauschäden wieder abgerissen werden. Dennoch beeinflussten diese Theorien die gesamte Stadt- und Wohnungsbauplanung der nächsten Jahrzehnte.

Ricardo Bofill/Taller de Arquitectura   Barrio Gaudi   Reus   Spain Spanien   1967

Superstructures implied risks, namely the loss of local specificities and of human scale. What had started as a search for democratic space often led to technical gigantism, as in the huge housing estates built by Ricardo Bofill/Taller de Arquitectura. While Bofill's earlier works (like the 1967 Barrio Gaudi in Reus) aimed at intimate communal living in big cities, his fortress-like Walden Seven Estate (1972) and the aptly-named Kafka's Castle (1968), both in Barcelona, are characterized by monumental forms dominating over residential qualities. Developments like these explain the growing critique of contemporary urban planning and housing in the late 1960s and 1970s.[5]

2   La Ville, 1994, pp. 430–31
3   Ibid., 1994, pp. 428–29
4   Ibid., 1994, pp. 434–35
5   C.f. e.g.: Mitscherlich, 1967

Zu den Risiken der Metastadt-Projekte gehörten der Verlust lokaler Besonderheiten und des menschlichen Maßstabs. An die Stelle ›demokratischer‹ Räume trat nicht selten technische Gigantomanie. Dies zeigt sich deutlich etwa in den Bauten von Ricardo Bofill/Taller de Arquitectura, wie der festungsartigen Anlage Walden Seven oder dem durchaus passend benannten Kafka's Castle, beide in Barcelona. Solche Entwicklungen machen die wachsende Kritik an der »Unwirtlichkeit unserer Städte« (Alexander Mitscherlich, 1967) verständlich.

Ricardo Bofill/Taller de Arquitectura   Kafka's Castle   Barcelona   Spain Spanien   1968

SOCIAL HOUSING IN THE USA   SOZIALER WOHNUNGSBAU IN DEN USA

Richard Meier & Partners
Twin Parks Northeast Housing
New York   New York, USA   1969–1974

The Twin Parks estate was part of an ambitious, state-run, social housing programme situated in the East Tremont section of the Bronx, an old Italian neighbourhood which had fallen into decay in the 1960s and was full of empty lots, closed stores, rubbish in the streets and, most fatally of all, marked by a rapidly increasing crime rate. In 1967 the Urban Design Group of the New York City Planning Commission carried out a study to define pockets of land for development throughout the borough. The Twin Parks Association, a non-profit, county-based company, commissioned several architects, among them Richard Meier, to draft plans for the integration of new residential buildings into the existing urban fabric. One aim was to provide a maximum of useable public space for the local community, another one to focus on infill housing situations to increase the density without the usual building clearance.

The site occupies parts of three adjacent city blocks with an irregular street pattern. The new buildings were to fit in to reinforce the existing street walls – a remarkably sensitive approach to maintain the character of a built-up area. Meier also employed dark brown tiles for the façades, their masonry texture relating the estate to the older brick buildings. In order to provide sufficient public space the ground floors are set back and the massive volumes rest on pillars. This enhances the physical continuity of the plaza below and unifies the three buildings, two of which are towers of sixteen storeys plus several lower blocks, overlooking a small park and the Bronx Zoo. In addition, the borough decided to close off traffic from the major outdoor space, Grote Street, to create a net of pedestrian ways through the district. Twin Parks Northeast focussed on area development rather than on isolated architecture. It incorporates

the existing city grid instead of destroying it, which had so often been the case in renewal schemes. Though clearly higher than their neighbours the different parts of the estate respect the quality and texture of the existing buildings and display a modern yet humane architectural vocabulary of flat façades, pilotis and flush metal windows.

Die in einem heruntergekommenen Gebiet der Bronx gelegenen Siedlungsbauten Twin Parks Northeast waren Teil eines ambitionierten Sozialwohnungsprogramms der Stadt New York. Ziel der gemeinnützigen Twin Parks Association war es, die Dichte durch Baulückenschließungen, aber ohne die üblichen Abbruchmaßnahmen zu erhöhen. Gleichzeitig sollten großzügige öffentliche Räume und ein Fußwegenetz durch das Gebiet entstehen. Die Gebäude erstrecken sich über drei Blöcke und stellten – bemerkenswert für die Zeit – die geschlossenen Straßenwände wieder her. Für die Fassaden verwendete Richard Meier dunkelbraune Fliesen, deren Textur auf die benachbarten Ziegelbauten verweist. Die massiven Bauten – zwei 16-stöckige Hochhäuser und mehrere niedrigere Trakte – ruhen auf Pilotis, wodurch weite öffentliche Bereiche und Durchgänge entstehen. Der Schwerpunkt der Planung liegt nicht auf isolierter Architektur, sondern auf behutsamer Einfügung in die bestehende städtische Struktur.

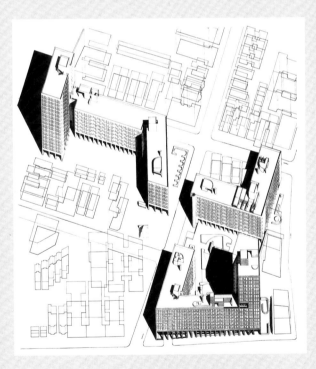

Richard Meier & Partners   Bronx Development Center   New York   USA   1970–1976

A few years later, Richard Meier planned another large building in the neighbourhood: the Bronx Developmental Center to serve as accommodation for 380 disabled children and to provide an outpatient facility. He designed a huge rectangular structure around closed courtyards which aims at expandability and flexibility. The Center became famous for its innovative, metal-panel cladding, a frequent element of industrial building, but never used in residential development before. The cladding is of anodized aluminium with the windows and vent openings punched out in the factory.[1] Unfortunately, this building, an 'often underestimated'[2] masterpiece of 1970s architecture which preceded the typically white walls of Meier's later designs, was severely altered in the course of recent renovation.

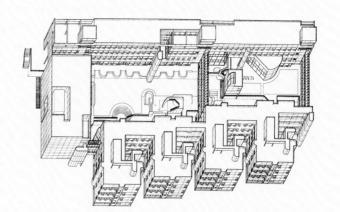

1   Meier, 1984, p. 138
2   Frampton, 2002, p. 11

Einige Jahre später baute Meier das in der Nähe gelegene **Bronx Developmental Center** für 380 behinderte Kinder. Es wurde vor allem durch seine innovative Fassade aus vorgefertigten Aluminiumpaneelen – ein Element des Industriebaus, das erstmals im Wohnungsbau Verwendung fand – berühmt. Leider wurde dieses Meisterstück der 1970er-Jahre Architektur, ein Vorgänger der weißen Häuser des Architekten, durch kürzlich erfolgte Renovierungsarbeiten empfindlich verändert.

Herman J. Jessor   Co-Op City   New York   USA   1968–1970

Such buildings were conceived as the generators of social and communal values, but remained rare exceptions in the US. Their socially oriented approach was not continued due to changing political priorities. The humane scale of the Twin Parks estates becomes even more noteworthy when compared to other contemporary social housing developments, such as the infamous Bronx Co-Op City (by Herman J. Jessor, 1968–70). Financed by several trade unions, Co-Op City included an incredible 15,372 flats for some 55,000 residents, squeezed into thirty-five tower blocks and 236 lower building parts. With its uniform brick façades it became a symbol of the failure of a housing policy which increasingly stigmatized social housing tenants and increased segregation in cities.

Sozialorientierte Bauten wie diese stellten seltene Ausnahmen im amerikanischen Wohnungsbau dar. Einerseits veränderten sich die politischen Prioritäten in den folgenden Jahren, andererseits führten Sozialwohnungsbauten wie die monotone Co-Op City von Herman J. Jessor (1968–1970), ebenfalls in der Bronx, mit nicht weniger als 15 372 Wohnungen für 55 000 Bewohner zur Stigmatisierung der sozial schwachen Mieter und damit zu einer verstärkten sozialen Segregation.

DOWNTOWN LIVING   INNERSTÄDTISCHES WOHNEN

Bertrand Goldberg
Marina City
Chicago   Illinois, USA   1959–1964

Overlooking the Chicago River, Marina City's two 179-metre-high towers, frequently referred to as the 'Corn Cobs', have long since become a landmark of downtown Chicago. At the time of construction they were the world's tallest residential buildings and the tallest concrete structures.[1] But, in fact, it was social concerns rather than architectural considerations which stood at the beginning of the planning process. In the early 1960s the future of American inner cities looked dim, with more and more middle-class workers moving to the suburbs. Therefore, the Chicago labour unions, trying to stop the urban flight of their members, supported Bertrand Goldberg's attempt to create a self-contained 'city within the city'. Consequently, Marina City accommodates not only nine-hundred apartments but also a wide range of shops, restaurants, offices, banks, two theatres, a gym, a pool, a skating rink, a large sculpture garden, and – of course – a marina.

Ironically, though, what the visitor sees first are cars. Each of the sixty-storey towers has a continuous parking ramp for 450 cars which extends over twenty levels. Thus, residential units start only at the twenty-first floor, providing each apartment with a magnificent view over Chicago's Loop, as the pie-shaped living rooms extend into rings of semicircular balconies. The towers are supported by a cylindrical reinforced concrete core which holds all the services and utilities. The construction of this core preceded that of the floors providing a rising foundation for the crane[2] and reducing the costs considerably. From a formal point of view, Marina City was the first high-rise development which did not adopt the right-angled 'Miesian' pattern – although Goldberg had studied at the Bauhaus and was a Mies van der Rohe apprentice. This search for new forms was no coincidence, however. Goldberg was also an engineer and had been involved in the development of pre-fabricated housing for the US government during WW II. Gradually he had developed a theory of kinetic space which would result in the use of circular forms – and, according to the architect, in more usable interior space, more direct mechanical distribution, more pre-fabricated elements and more efficient wind resistance. Moreover, Goldberg considered rectilinear shapes opposed to human activity, the post-and-beam structures being a 'hangover from Victorian tradition'.[3]

Marina City was the culmination of thirty years of research but found no successors – probably because it took place outside the predominant academic mainstream. What remained is the courageous attempt at inner-city revival, a vibrant multi-purpose complex which after forty years still satisfies a high-

standard, middle-class lifestyle, and one of the most individualistic designs ever achieved in reinforced concrete – at least in the housing sector. "Marina City transformed the aesthetics of reinforced concrete and blew a breath of lyricism into contemporary architecture."[4]

1 Wright, 1989, p. 36
2 Heyer, 1966, p. 52
3 Goldberg, from: Heyer, 1966, p. 49
4 Dupré, 1996, p. 59

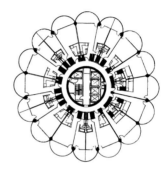

Die zwei oft als ›Maiskolben‹ bezeichneten, 179 Meter hohen Türme der Marina City waren zum Zeitpunkt ihrer Erbauung die höchsten Wohngebäude und die höchsten Betonkonstruktionen der Welt. Sie stellten den Versuch dar, durch eine eigenständige ›Stadt in der Stadt‹ der Verödung des Zentrums von Chicago entgegenzuwirken. Daher umfasst Marina City neben 900 Wohnungen auch Büros und ein umfangreiches Angebot an Freizeiteinrichtungen. Der erste Blick fällt allerdings auf Autos: In jedem der 60-geschossigen Türme werden die untersten 20 Geschosse von einer rampenförmig ansteigenden Garage eingenommen. Die Wohnungen ab dem 21. Stock öffnen sich zu halbkreisförmigen Balkonen mit prachtvollem Blick auf den Loop, Chicagos Innenstadt. Die tragende Konstruktion des Stahlbetonkerns wurde jeweils vor den entsprechenden Geschossen errichtet, um eine stetig steigende Plattform für den Montagekran zu schaffen und dadurch die Baukosten zu senken. Formal vollzog Goldberg mit der Marina City eine Abkehr von der rechtwinkeligen Stahlbetonarchitektur seines Lehrers Mies van der Rohe. Seinen Studien kinetischer Räume zufolge sollten zylindrische Formen zu mehr Nutzfläche, besserer Kräfteverteilung, mehr vorgefertigten Elementen und höherer Windresistenz führen. Marina City blieb dennoch ohne Nachfolger – vermutlich, weil sie zu sehr außerhalb der vorherrschenden akademischen Lehre stand. Was bleibt, ist der erfolgreiche Versuch einer Revitalisierung der Innenstadt und die einzigartige, zumindest im Wohnungsbau kaum jemals wieder erreichte Individualität der Stahlbetonarchitektur.

CARIBBEAN LIGHTNESS   KARIBISCHE LEICHTIGKEIT

Arquitectonica
The Atlantis Condominium Apartmentblock The Atlantis
Miami   Florida, USA   1980–1982

Arquitectonica, today with a staff of over 300 and with offices in the US, Asia, Europe and South America, was founded as a small firm in 1977. In spite of projects all over the world it soon became associated with Florida. Indeed, some of their smaller condominiums recall the landmark buildings from Miami's Art Deco period – not so much in their design details but rather in the overall treatment of volumes, the relation to the tropical surroundings and, last but not least, the use of lively, 'Caribbean' colour schemes. It was the huge Atlantis condominium, however, which became a symbol of tropical modernism as well as of the revival of downtown Miami in the late 1970s.

Situated at the prestigious Biscayne Bay, the twenty-storey slab building contains ninety-five up-market condominiums, in-

cluding duplex apartments with double-height living rooms and private gardens at the base. It does not hide its dimensions but rather emphasizes them through its self-conscious design. The imposing 100-metre-long block is topped by geometric volumes – cubes and a pyramid concealing the mechanical equipment on the flat roof, and the east side facing the bay is shaped like a nautical curve providing the living rooms with a 180-degree view. On the south side, the glass wall is covered by a three-storey masonry grid that shades the cantilevered balconies while the reflective glass of the northern façade is punctuated by four yellow triangular balconies. What gives the building its truly unique character, however, is the four-storey cube which is cut out at the centre of the slab. This 'sky court' with its palm tree,

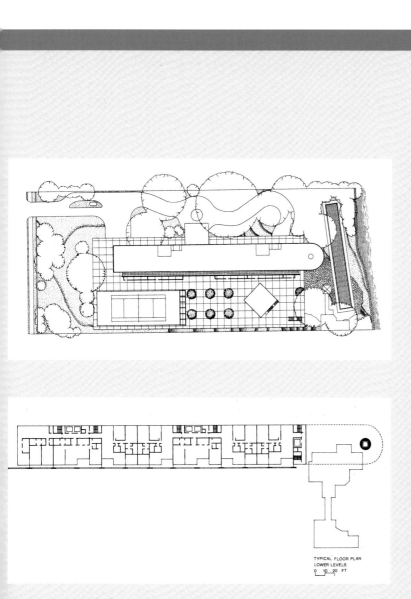

TYPICAL FLOOR PLAN
LOWER LEVELS
0   10   20   FT

red corkscrew staircase and blue pool offers astounding vistas both from the building itself and from outside. The lively colours further underline the dialogue between the building and its tropical environment. With the Atlantis Apartments, Arquitectonica created a new type of a luxury condominium complex which was to become the model for a large number of similar – if often less carefully designed – developments in coastal areas.

Das Architekturbüro Arquitectonica, das heute weltweit tätig ist, wurde vor allem durch seine Bauten in Miami bekannt, die in der Gestaltung der Baukörper, ihrer Beziehung zur Umgebung und der

›karibischen‹ Farbgebung an die dortige Art-Déco-Architektur erinnern und zum Symbol eines tropischen Modernismus wurden. Der 20-stöckige Wohnblock The Atlantis, an der prestigeträchtigen Biscayne Bay gelegen, zeichnet sich durch eine selbstbewusste geometrische Form, kubische und pyramidenförmige Dachaufbauten, vor allem aber durch den herausgestanzten vierstöckigen ›sky court‹ im 9. Stock mit Terrasse, Palme und Pool aus. Vielfältige Durchblicke und die lebhaften Farben unterstreichen den spannungsreichen Dialog zwischen Gebäude und tropischer Natur. Mit den Atlantis-Apartments schuf Arquitectonica einen neuen Typus von Luxuswohnanlage, der zum Vorbild zahlreicher – wenngleich oft weit weniger sorgfältig geplanter – Anlagen in Küstengebieten wurde.

Arquitectonica further developed their design approach which is based on the use of simple geometric forms on a large scale in buildings such as the stunning forty-two-storey The Palace Condominium, again at Biscayne Bay, downtown Miami. The firm's first experience into the idea of the three-dimensional collage resulted in two buildings, the lower one with stepped terraces virtually cutting through the higher block and reappearing on the other side as a monumental gate. Each unit profits from view of both the city and the bay, with additional townhouses lining a waterfront promenade. The aim is clear: to create identity, or at least the illusion of it, for each of the 265 condominium units within one large estate – the dramatic architecture becoming part of a marketing strategy[1] in an increasingly competitive housing market segment.

1   Ravettlat, 1992, p. 73, notices the 'film set' element of these buildings which may be responsible for their being used as locations in numerous TV commercials and films

Arquitectonica selbst machten mit Gebäuden wie dem beeindruckenden 42-stöckigen The Palace Condominium in Miami, einer dreidimensionalen Collage aus einander durchdringenden Baukörpern, Architektur zum Marketinginstrument in einem zunehmend umkämpften Wohnungsmarktsegment.

Arquitectonica   The Palace   Miami, Florida   USA   1979–1982

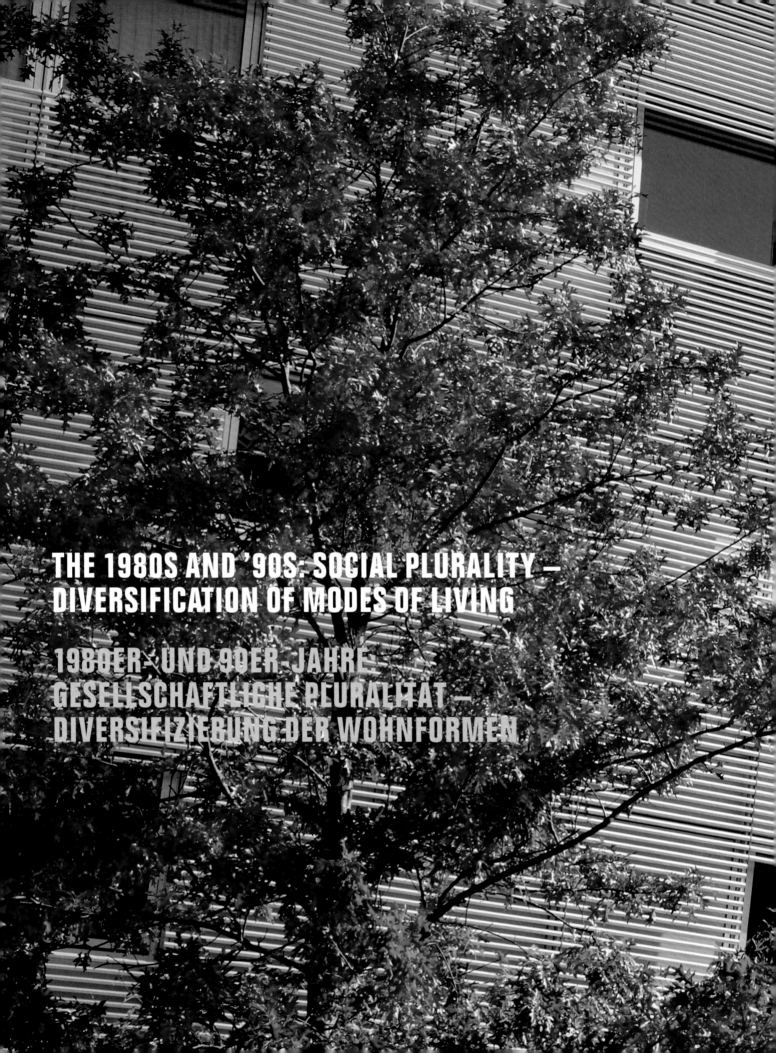

THE 1980S AND '90S: SOCIAL PLURALITY – DIVERSIFICATION OF MODES OF LIVING

1980ER- UND 90ER-JAHRE: GESELLSCHAFTLICHE PLURALITÄT – DIVERSIFIZIERUNG DER WOHNFORMEN

ARCHITECTURE AS SOCIAL RESPONSIBILITY
ARCHITEKTUR ALS GESELLSCHAFTLICHE VERANTWORTUNG

Ralph Erskine
Myrstuguberget
Stockholm   Sweden Schweden   1985–1988

Ralph Erskine designed a number of housing estates in England where he had been influenced by the theories of garden city development and by the post-war British neighbourhood planning approach. However, it was in Scandinavia where he was best able to realize his ideas of contemporary social housing. Erskine was fascinated by the challenge of housing construction in the extreme north, resulting in several stunning residential schemes in Canada and Lapland. In these projects he studied the indigenous way of life north of the Arctic circle and its effects on architecture. His credo that under such extreme circumstances 'form follows climate'[1] led him to study the consequences of different types of roofs, façades, shutters, etc. for the interior climate of buildings. Balconies, for example, should be suspended from the roof instead of being cantilevered from

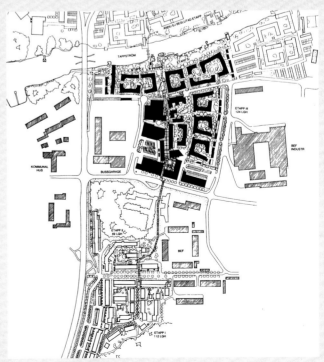

the walls in order to avoid cold conduction, while on a much larger scale, whole high-latitude towns could be sheltered by gigantic domes.[2] At the same time, Erskine was also deeply impressed by the Swedish welfare-state model which, for the first time, promised to provide access to high-standard housing for everybody.

Erskine's first large housing estate in Stockholm became the physical expression of his earlier studies. Situated on a rocky plateau about fifty metres above its surroundings, Myrstuguberget includes 411 apartments. The plan makes optimum use of this difficult topography by arranging most of the flats in two long blocks, the southern one profiting from a beautiful view over Lake Mälaren, the northern one sheltering the low-rise housing. In a dramatic gesture, the development of the western wing follows the steep incline to the lake, with the number of levels increasing from seven to eleven. The whole area is traffic-free, with pleasant and protected paths for pedestrians. The scheme includes a school centre and a day-care centre. Erskine was obviously not happy with some of the details – notably the 'totally uncultivated' aluminium balcony railings[3] – but the estate, with its characteristic silhouette seen from the lake, remains a remarkable monument both to his humanistic planning approach and to the socially oriented, Swedish, post-war housing policy.

1 Egelius, 1990, p. 68
2 Collymore, 1982, pp. 27–30
3 Egelius, 1990, p. 187

Ralph Erskine hatte schon einige Wohnkomplexe in England entworfen und sich vor allem intensiv mit der Herausforderung zeitgemäßen Wohnens in arktischen Regionen beschäftigt, bevor er 1985 die erste große Wohnhausanlage in Stockholm plante. Die 411 Wohnungen in Myrstuguberget, einem felsigen Plateau 50 Meter über dem Mälarsee, sind in mehreren langen Zeilen angeordnet. Diese gewähren den bestmöglichen Ausblick auf den See, aber auch Schutz vor dem Nordwind. Dramatisch wirkt die dem steilen Hang folgende Bebauung im westlichen Teil der Anlage, die auch ein Schulzentrum beherbergt. Erskine war über einige Ausführungsdetails nicht glücklich, dennoch stellt der Wohnkomplex mit seiner weithin sichtbaren charakteristischen Silhouette ein Denkmal seines humanistischen Planungsansatzes und zugleich der sozial orientierten schwedischen Wohnungspolitik der Nachkriegszeit dar.

Architectuurstudio Herman Hertzberger   **Rotterdamstrasse**   **Düren**   **Germany** Deutschland   **1993–1996**

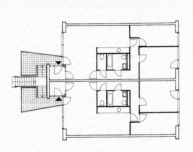

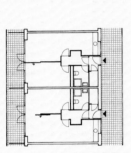

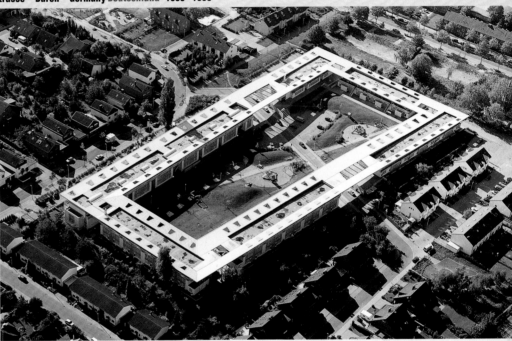

Among those architects who have always given a high priority to social considerations and to planning on a human scale is Herman Hertzberger. Most of his housing projects are based on the Dutch 'Building the Neighbourhood' approach. When designing the new housing estate, Rotterdamstrasse in Düren, Germany (1993–96) he insisted on abolishing the existing land-use plan with its scattered single-family housing. Instead, three-storey units are arranged along the perimeter of the site, with a large green courtyard accessible from all sides. A dominant, protruding roof, which also serves as a sun shade, unifies the complex, providing identity within the rather dismal suburb without destroying its scale and character.

Zu jenen Architekten, die sozialen Überlegungen immer hohe Priorität einräumten, gehört der Holländer **Herman Hertzberger**. In der **Wohnhausanlage Rotterdamerstraße** in **Düren** (1993–1996) ersetzte er die vorgesehene formlose Verbauung mit Einfamilienhäusern durch dreistöckige Zeilen um einen öffentlich zugänglichen, begrünten Innenhof. Ein einheitliches, weit vorkragendes Dach wirkt identitätsstiftend, ohne den Maßstab und den Charakter des Vororts zu zerstören.

REPAIRING THE CITY   STADTREPARATUR

Aldo Rossi, Oswald Mathias Ungers
International Building Exhibition Internationale Bauausstellung
Berlin   Germany Deutschland   1987

In 1979, the West-Berlin Senate decided to hold the International Building Exhibition (IBA) in 1987 and commissioned the architect Josef Paul Kleihues with the organization. The exhibition should consist of three parts: 'gentle urban renewal', 'urban reconstruction' in the southern part of Friedrichstadt which had been destroyed during the war and as a result of the division of Berlin, and 'city repair' in the Tiergarten district. New housing construction was mainly to take place in Friedrichstadt and Tiergarten while the renewal programme was focussed on housing refurbishment in the Kreuzberg district. Kleihues concentrated on urban planning rather than on single projects[1] and he wanted to rediscover the order of the historic city by way of a 'critical reconstruction' rather than by 'post-modernist illusion'. The new housing estates should, therefore, be characterized by a dialogue between tradition and modernism. Most of them were

built within the subsidized social housing system, either as in-fills to conceal the scars left by the war, or as larger developments in the place of bombed city blocks. However, given the damage caused by earlier reconstruction schemes based on the ideal of a low-density city with isolated buildings in an open, urban landscape, there seemed to be only one option for a critical reconstruction: the 19th-century grid pattern with buildings of uniform height surrounding inner courtyards. This considerably limited the freedom of the planners, including most of the architectural élite of the 1980s.

In spite of this restrictive planning approach there are some remarkable examples of inner-city housing. Aldo Rossi won the Kochstrasse/Friedrichstrasse competition which focussed on new formulations for block corners but it seems that he more mocked than respected the austere Berlin grid structure. The

long façades are interrupted by staircases topped by steep gables reminiscent of medieval German towns, while the corner dissolves into a huge column. The colouring is lively with a dominant brick red. The courtyard is carefully landscaped and visually open to passers-by. Rossi deliberately plays with the various relations between the classicist uniformity of the old city structure and the individual housing scheme.

1   Bauausstellung Berlin GmbH, 1987, p. 6

Der West-Berliner Senat beauftragte 1979 Josef Paul Kleihues mit der Organisation einer Internationalen Bauausstellung (IBA) im Jahr 1987. Diese sollte aus drei Teilen bestehen: der »behutsamen Stadterneuerung«, der »Stadtrekonstruktion« und der »Stadtreparatur«. Kleihues stellte dabei die städtebauliche Planung in den Vordergrund, nicht das Einzelprojekt. Die Gesetzmäßigkeiten der historischen Stadt sollten durch kritische Rekonstruktion in einem Dialog zwischen Tradition und Moderne wieder entdeckt werden. Das verbindliche Modell dafür war der geschlossene Block des 19. Jahrhunderts. Innerhalb dieses engen Konzepts entstanden einige bemerkenswerte Wohnungsbauten wie der Bau Kochstraße/Friedrichstraße von Aldo Rossi, der eine städtebauliche Neuformulierung der Blockecken anstrebte. Rossi ironisierte diese Vorgaben durch steile, an mittelalterliche deutsche Städte erinnernde Giebel und lebhafte Farben.

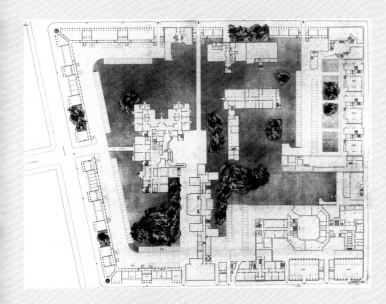

Aldo Rossi's housing estate on Kochstrasse/Friedrichstrasse
Aldo Rossis Wohnbau an der Kochstraße/Friedrichstraße

Housing block by Oswald Mathias Ungers on Köthener Strasse   Wohnblock von Oswald Mathias Ungers an der Köthener Straße

Probably the strongest architectural statement comes from the massive block by Oswald Mathias Ungers on Köthener Strasse. Eight towers, connected to each other at the upper half of the six-storey building, create a fortress-like structure on this forty-by-forty-metre parcel. Ungers emphasizes the Berlin grid pattern by extending it to the whole plan and even to the façades. Each flat occupies the whole level of one tower, thus facing out on all four sides. Floor plans are generous, as the forty-five flats were built for larger families. In spite of its monumental appearance the cubic block communicates strongly with its surroundings, the three-storey-high openings between the towers inviting passers-by to stroll through the courtyard.

Die wahrscheinlich stärkste architektonische Aussage liefert die festungsartige Anlage von Oswald Mathias Ungers an der Köthener Straße. Ungers übertrug den Blockraster auf den gesamten Bau einschließlich der Fassaden. Die großzügig angelegten Wohnungen sind nach vier Seiten orientiert, der Innenhof ist öffentlich zugänglich.

Rob Krier   Ritterstrasse   Berlin   Germany Deutschland   1977–1980

Among the IBA buildings most discussed at the time were two estates based on master plans by Rob Krier. In the Tiergarten district Krier developed an area of 'urban villas' (*Stadtvillen*) which, in fact, are five-storey apartment blocks of identical size. Hans Hollein was one of the architects. Krier's own building consists of two such blocks connected by an arched wing which has been described as being reminiscent of the Karl-Marx-Hof estate in Vienna from the 1920s. Flats with tiny, irregular rooms are squeezed into a dominant, symmetrical form. More than any other IBA development this showed that urban reconstruction did not automatically lead to new housing solutions. The second plan by Rob Krier was for the Ritterstrasse Estate. Here several blocks – again with a huge, arched gate – surround pleasant, landscaped courtyards creating a net of pedestrian paths through the whole area. However, the floor-plans are even worse than in Tiergarten and the post-modernist architecture culminates at the pseudo-classical Schinkel Square.

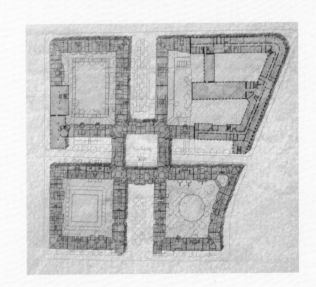

Zu den meistdiskutierten IBA-Planungen gehören zwei Wohnhausanlagen von **Rob Krier**: die Stadtvillen im Tiergartenviertel und die Anlage **Ritterstraße**. Bei den Stadtvillen, die unter anderem von **Hans Hollein** entworfen wurden, handelt es sich eigentlich um sechsgeschossige Wohnblocks. Krier selbst zwängte enge, unregelmäßige Wohnräume in zwanghaft symmetrische Baukörper, insbesondere am pseudoklassizistischen Schinkelplatz.

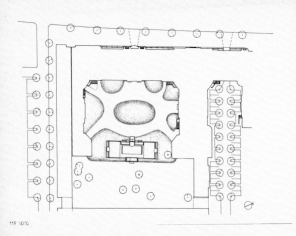

Arata Isozaki & Associates **Lindenstrasse** **Berlin** **Germany Deutschland** **1982–1986**

Gregotti Associati **Lützowstrasse** **Berlin** **Germany Deutschland** **1986**

Other notable IBA developments include the Lindenstrasse Estate with excellent housing by **Hans Kollhoff** and **Arata Isozaki**, the nearby participatory planning project by **Herman Hertzberger** and the impressive housing scheme by **Vittorio Gregotti** on Lützowstrasse. Almost twenty years later – and after political events which completely changed the face of Berlin but could not have been foreseen in 1987 – what is still impressive is the uniquely comprehensive approach to inner-city living. The individual buildings paint a different picture. Some of them are convincingly metropolitan, others simply post-modernist kitsch. The 'city repair' was a success; Kleihues and his team understood that such a scheme had to be strongly process-oriented, taking into account the very specific dynamics of (West) Berlin. It was the 'gentle' refurbishment model with its tenants' participation, however, which influenced urban renewal all over the world. But that is a story to be told in another context.

Bemerkenswerte Wohnungsbauten planten auch **Hans Kollhoff** und **Arata Isozaki**, Herman Hertzberger (ein Mietermitbestimmungsprojekt) und **Vittorio Gregotti**. Im Rückblick nach 20 Jahren beeindruckt noch immer der umfassende Planungsansatz. Die Architektur erscheint zwiespältig – zum Teil überzeugend großstädtisch, zum Teil schlicht postmoderner Kitsch. Gelungen ist jedenfalls die Stadtreparatur, weil Kleihues deren Prozesscharakter in der sehr spezifischen Dynamik (West-) Berlins begründete. Es war jedoch die behutsame Stadterneuerung, die ähnliche Programme weltweit beeinflusste – eine Geschichte, die in einem ganz anderen Konnex zu diskutieren wäre.

Architectuurstudio Herman Hertzberger **LiMa Housing** **Berlin** **Germany** Deutschland **1982–1986**

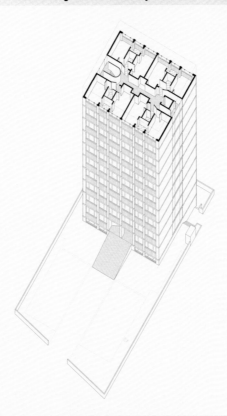

Colquhoun + Miller **Hornsey Lane** **London** **Great Britain** Großbritannien **1980**

The discussion of city repair, started in the late 1970s, led to a number of interesting projects all over Europe. Among them is the very carefully planned Hornsey Lane housing estate by Alan Colquhoun and John Miller at Haringey, London (1980) which – similar to the IBA developments – returns to planning on a human scale. The cubic, nine-storey block is a reminder of Ungers' later building in Berlin, yet it remains typically 'British' in its dialogue with the adjacent residential area.

Zu den zahlreichen Stadtreparatur-Projekten in Europa, die eine Rückkehr zum menschlichen Maßstab anstrebten, gehört auch die besonders sorgfältig geplante Anlage in der Hornsey Lane von Alan Colquhoun und John Miller in Haringey, London (1980).

HOUSING IN THE MEGACITY   WOHNEN IN DER MEGASTADT

Mark Mack
Nexus Housing Wohnanlage Nexus
Fukuoka   Japan   1989–1991

Mark Mack was invited to design a multi-storey residential scheme within a large new development in the Japanese town of Fukuoka. The master plan came from Arata Isozaki and other well-known architects such as Arquitectonica, Steven Holl, Rem Koolhaas and Christian de Portzamparc participated in the project. While Isozaki designed the high-rise buildings in the middle of the rectangular plot, the other architects received identical pieces of land at the perimeter of the site.[1] This was Mack's first project in Asia and it is interesting to analyze how he adapted the principles of his earlier Californian houses – most of them up-market, private residences – to the specific situation in this densely built-up boom town. First of all, Mack applied their highly individual architecture to this large housing complex: each of the twenty-nine apartments is unique and this is clearly expressed by the façades with their irregular distribution of windows, balconies and panel elements. Some flats have private roof terraces or small allotment-gardens in the courtyard. The build-

ing consists of two wings, the higher concrete-frame slab resting on the lower block which is painted bright red. The lively colour scheme is continued in the interior spaces.

But it is inside the apartments where the ingeniously designed floor plans best display the refreshingly new approach to multi-family housing – and a very Japanese approach at that. Although individual dwellings are small (at least by European or American standards) they appear spacious due to the masterful treatment of volumes and materials. The layout of the two-storey units draws upon the 'Raumplan' – a three-dimensional design model – by Adolf Loos in Vienna where Mark had studied. Unlike Loos, however, Mark employs cheap materials like brightly stained plywood panelling for the walls and built-in furniture. These elements refer back to traditional Japanese architecture as do the sliding doors and the *tatami* rooms in the atrium units.

1   Ghirardo, 1994, p. 133

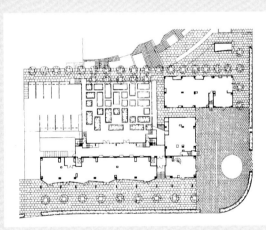

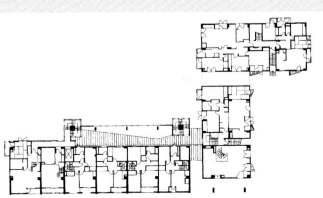

Mark Mack wurde von Arata Isozaki eingeladen, gemeinsam mit mehreren Architekten aus Japan, Europa und den USA ein Wohngebiet in Fukuoka zu planen. In seinem ersten asiatischen Projekt überträgt Mack die individuelle Architektur seiner luxuriösen Häuser in Kalifornien auf einen mehrgeschossigen Wohnbau, indem er die Verschiedenheit der insgesamt 29 Wohnungen an der Fassade deutlich ablesbar macht: Fenster, Balkone und Platten sind völlig unregelmäßig angeordnet. Der höhere der beiden Blöcke ruht mit seinem sichtbaren Stahlbetonrahmen auf einem niedrigeren roten Baukörper. Diese lebhafte Farbgebung setzt sich in den Innenräumen fort. Ein erfrischend neuer Zugang zum mehrgeschossigen Wohnungsbau zeigt sich aber vor allem in den Wohnungsgrundrissen. Durch den meisterhaften Umgang mit Volumina und Materialien scheinen die Wohnungen größer als sie eigentlich sind; die zweigeschossigen Einheiten erinnern an den Raumplan von Adolf Loos. Anders als Loos verwendet Mack aber kostengünstige Materialien, darunter verschiedenfarbig lasierte Sperrholzplatten für Innenwände und Einbaumöbel. Wie die Schiebetüren und die Tatami-Räume nehmen sie auf traditionelle japanische Architekturelemente Bezug.

Stanley Tigerman Momochi Residential Complex **Wohnkomplex Momochi** Fukuoka Japan 1988–1991

Another exciting project at Fukuoka was designed by Stanley Tigerman at the Momochi Residential Complex (1988–91). The layered elements of the six-storeyed façades re-interpret vernacular Japanese residential architecture while open galleries create a strong abstract pattern on the courtyard walls.

Ein weiteres ungewöhnliches Wohngebäude in Fukuoka, der Wohnkomplex Momochi (1988–1991), wurde von **Stanley Tigerman** geplant. Die Schichtung der sechsstöckigen Fassade erinnert ebenfalls an die klassische japanische Architektur.

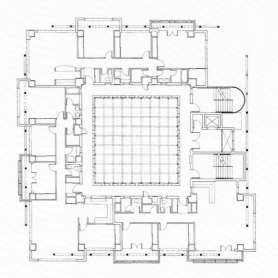

Francisco Javier Sáenz de Oiza   Polígono 38   Madrid   Spain Spanien   1986–1990

All over the world city planners and architects have increasingly been facing the same challenge: to provide intimacy and identity within seemingly endless urban agglomerations. This particularly concerns middle-class housing, situated somehow between the extremes of monotonous housing complexes for low-income households and gated communities for the well-off. In Mexico City the office of Legorreta Arquitectos designed a convincing example of inner-city housing with the Pasaje Santa Fe complex (1995). Several lively coloured buildings surround semi-public atriums, passages and internal squares, aiming at recovering the community life in this old metropolitan neighbourhood.[2] The complex includes sixty-two apartments on the four upper levels and a number of restaurants on the ground floor. Similarly, the Polígono 38 estate (1986–90) in Madrid by Francisco Javier Sáenz de Oiza aims at intimate housing by one of the city's busiest motorways. The huge complex curves in a spiral around a large courtyard, the height alternating between four and eight storeys. Its monochrome exterior wall with small windows contrasts sharply with the colourist design of the inner façades.

2   Broto, 2004, p. 340

Weltweit sehen sich heute Städteplaner und Architekten mit der Herausforderung konfrontiert, Intimität und Identität in den endlos wuchernden urbanen Agglomerationen zu schaffen. Dies betrifft vor allem das Wohnen der Mittelklasse, das irgendwo zwischen monotonen Sozialwohnungsbauten und teuren Gated Communities angesiedelt ist. In Mexiko-Stadt schuf das Büro Legorreta Arquitectos mit dem Komplex Pasaje Santa Fe (1995) ein beeindruckendes Beispiel für innerstädtisches Wohnen. Ähnlich bietet die riesige, gekurvte Wohnanlage Polígono 38 (1986–1990) in Madrid von Francisco Javier Sáenz de Oiza die Möglichkeit zurückgezogenen Wohnens an einer der frequentiertesten Straßen der Stadt.

SPACE AS TRUE LUXURY   RAUM ALS LUXUS

Ateliers Jean Nouvel
Nemausus 1
Nîmes   France Frankreich   1985–1987

Social housing development in Europe has been increasingly confronted with a double challenge: the avoidance of creating social ghettoes, meaning that the development should not be concentrated around the less attractive fringe areas, and rising land prices in the more prestigious inner-cities districts. If housing for the less privileged is still to be constructed in such areas, two options seem realistic – the density of such estates must be increased and/or building costs reduced. In the groundbreaking Nemausus 1 estate in Nîmes, Jean Nouvel clearly focussed on the second solution.

Nemausus 1 was built as part of the Nîmes social housing programme in an industrial zone. It contains 114 apartments in two parallel, six-storey blocks and, as most of them are duplex apartments, corridors are only needed on every second level. This reduces access space within the useable surface area, as do the open staircases on the exterior of the blocks. All apart-

ments are oriented to two sides, leading to broad communal corridors which can also be used as terraces. The reinforced concrete structure is based on a five-by-twelve metre grid. Floor plans are simple rectangles arranged in an additive pattern between the parallel galleries, providing no less than seventeen different house types. The main reason for cost reduction results from the consequent use of industrial materials: metal staircases, industrial flooring, perforated metal balustrades, PVC sunshades, marine lighting and – probably most shocking – large garage doors onto the corridors. The long blocks are topped by a dominant protruding roof of sheet metal which adds to the machine or ship-like impression. Car parking is on the ground floor as the buildings stand on pilotis.

This uncompromising technical approach to a social housing scheme may seem problematic or even cynical, given the economic situation of its underprivileged residents who have no

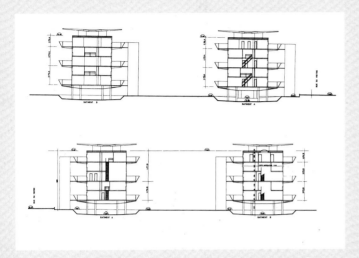

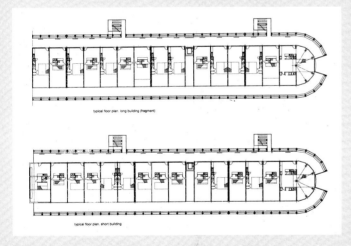

typical floor plan. long building (fragment)

typical floor plan. short building

other choice. Will they feel safe with open staircases and corridors? Do they really want to enter their dwellings through garage doors and to access their bedrooms via metal stairs along naked concrete walls? But, on the other hand, the adoption of industrial techniques and materials allows for more space at the same cost. Indeed, the apartments are spacious, and the useable floor area is – at least visually – increased by the large openings to the galleries. Even more importantly, the transparency of the ground floor and the very careful landscaping between and around the blocks create the impression of a garden city rather than of an industrial suburb. It remains to be seen if this kind of architecture will be accepted by future tenants (also depending, probably, on such conditions as the quality of maintenance and the overall security in the area). However, within the strict context of French social housing, Nouvel has presented a strikingly new approach which focuses on spatial qualities rather than 'unnecessary' material luxury.

Der soziale Wohnungsbau in Europa ist zunehmend mit der Herausforderung konfrontiert, trotz steigender Bodenpreise in attraktiveren Lagen soziale Ghettos zu vermeiden. Zwei Lösungen bieten sich an: die Dichte in solchen Anlagen zu erhöhen oder die Baukosten zu senken. Beim Projekt Nemausus 1 in Nîmes wählte Jean Nouvel die zweite Option. Die 114 Sozialwohnungen in einem Industrieviertel von Nîmes wurden in zwei parallelen, sechsgeschossigen Blöcken errichtet. Zwischen zwei offenen Gängen additiv angeordnet, bieten sie nicht weniger als 17 verschiedene Grundrisse. Nouvel verwendete konsequent Industriematerialen: außenliegende Metalltreppen, Industrieböden, Me-

tallgeländer, PVC-Sonnensegel, Schiffslampen und Garagentore als Eingänge zu den Wohnungen. Das mag angesichts der sozialen Situation der Bewohner, die kaum eine andere Wahl haben, problematisch oder sogar zynisch erscheinen, andererseits erlauben die Kosteneinsparungen großzügigere Grundrisse und eine sorgfältige Grünraumgestaltung. Es bleibt abzuwarten, ob eine solche Architektur auch von späteren Mietern akzeptiert wird. Nouvel hat jedenfalls innerhalb der engen Grenzen des französischen Sozialwohnungssystems einen völlig neuen Weg gewählt – mit der Betonung räumlicher Qualitäten anstelle eines ›unnötigen‹ materiellen Luxus.

MVRDV   100 WoZoCo'S   Amsterdam   The Netherlands Niederlande   1994–1997

In the Netherlands, the country in Europe with the greatest number of inhabitants per square kilometre, high occupation density has always been understood as a necessity to preserve valuable open spaces. When MVRDV were commissioned to plan 100 apartments for elderly residents in Amsterdam-Osdorp, a traditional garden city area, it soon turned out that only eighty-seven could be constructed without reducing the level of sunlight required for the surrounding buildings. At 100 WoZoCo'S (1994–97) MVRDV offered a surprising solution: the remaining thirteen units are suspended from the north façade by steel cantilever girders, providing each apartment with an east or west orientation (north-facing flats not being permitted in the Netherlands). The party walls, with sound insulation that is eight centimetres thicker than structurally necessary, take up the connection of the cantilever trusses. Furthermore, the economic layout of the main block with long access galleries reduced the construction costs by eight per cent to compensate for the more expensive suspended units. Flats have their own character due to varied window positions, balcony sizes and the use of different colours. The overhanging boxes not only give a striking presence at street level but also keep the ground floor as open and green as possible – a prototypical yet acceptable increase in density in such urban areas.

In den Niederlanden, dem am dichtesten besiedelten Land Europas, wurde hohe Wohndichte zur Erhaltung des wertvollen Grünlands immer schon akzeptiert. In der Wohnhausanlage 100 WoZoCo'S (1994–1997) in Amsterdam-Osdorp, einem Gartenstadtbezirk, konnten von den geplanten 100 Seniorenwohnungen aus Belichtungsgründen zunächst nur 87 untergebracht werden. MVRDV ordneten daher 13 Wohnungen in weit auskragenden Baukörpern auf Stahlträgern an der Nordfassade an. Die höheren Baukosten für diese Einheiten wurden durch Kosteneinsparungen beim Hauptblock mit seinen langen Laubengängen kompensiert. Wechselnde Fensteranordnungen, Balkongrößen und Farben geben den einzelnen Wohnungen Individualität. Die hängenden Boxen sorgen für ein auffallendes Erscheinungsbild, vor allem aber für die Freihaltung weiterer Grundflächen – ein prototypischer Ansatz zu höherer Dichte in städtischen Gebieten.

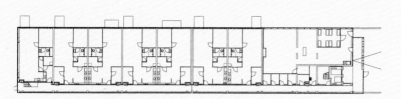

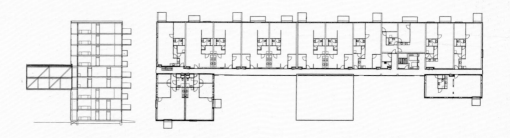

ARCHITECTURE OF THE NEW WORLD   ARCHITEKTUR DER NEUEN WELT

Harry Seidler & Associates
Horizon Apartments
Darlinghurst, Sydney   **Australia** Australien   **1990–1998**

This residential tower stands out from among the homogeneous grid of Victorian suburban terraces in the lively area of Darlinghurst which overlooks Sydney's Woolloomooloo Bay. It was created due to an exemption from local height restrictions; Harry Seidler successfully argued that a solitary tower would be less of an obstruction to views and sunlight than a building half the height and twice the footprint.[1] The forty-three-storey building overlooks a rectangular garden with swimming pool and tennis court and a number of smaller town houses.

Views are the principal determining factors. As a consequence, the tower is shaped as an arc opening to the west, north and east, providing all apartments with dramatic vistas to the Central Business District (with several of Seidler's office towers), the Sydney Harbour Bridge, the Opera House and the Tasman Sea. All living areas have full floor-to-ceiling glass walls. Balconies change from level to level to give shade to the floor below, adding a human scale to the high-rise, their rhythm of curving lines creating the sensation of waves glittering under the Southern sun and making the building easily recognizable from a distance. The organic plasticity which is typical for Seidler's later projects has been interpreted as 'a reworking of the tectonic order of the Bauhaus'[2] which influenced him when working with Walter Gropius and Marcel Breuer.

Apartments range from studios to spacious penthouse units. The double-height entrance atrium features black marble floors, Mies' Barcelona chairs and a large Op-art work by Sol Lewitt. The careful choice of materials further underlines the elegant character of this up-market development. It is interesting to note that Seidler planned another residential estate – including a 100-metre tower – with similarly high qualities within a social housing scheme in his native city Vienna, Austria, completed in 2001.[3]

1 Architectural Review, June 2001, p. 52
2 Frampton, 1992
3 see: Förster, 2002

Das Hochhaus der Horizon Apartments ragt aus dem einheitlichen Raster viktorianischer Reihenhäuser im lebhaften Bezirk Darlinghurst in Sydney heraus und verdankt seine Entstehung einer Ausnahme von der lokalen Beschränkung der Bauhöhen. Harry Seidler argumentierte erfolgreich, dass ein einzelnes Hochhaus den Ausblick und den Lichteinfall weniger beeinträchtigen würde als ein niedrigeres Gebäude auf größerer Grundfläche. Der bogenförmige Grundriss und die raumhohen Glaswände ermöglichen großartige Ausblicke über Sydney. Wechselseitig angeordnete Balkone bieten Schatten und erzeugen zugleich ein bewegtes, das Gebäude weithin erkennbar machendes Wellenmuster. Diese für Seidlers Spätwerk typische organische Plastizität wurde von Kenneth Frampton »als Überwindung der vom Bauhaus geprägten tektonischen Ordnung« interpretiert. Gleichermaßen sorgfältig ist die Materialauswahl, etwa in der eleganten zweigeschossigen Eingangshalle mit schwarzem Marmor, Barcelona-Sesseln von Mies van der Rohe und einem Op-Art-Kunstwerk von Sol Lewitt. All das unterstreicht den luxuriösen Charakter der Horizon Apartments. Bemerkenswert ist daher, dass Seidler 2001 in Wien, seiner Geburtsstadt, eine ähnliche Wohnhausanlage errichtete – diesmal jedoch innerhalb des sozialen Wohnbauprogramms.

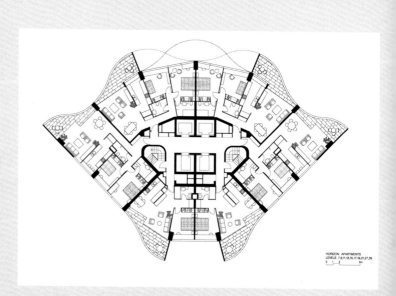

LIVING

BEDROOMS

LIVING

BEDROOMS

BEDROOMS

LIVING

LIVING

BEDROOMS

LIVING

LIVING

BEDROOMS

LIVING

LIVING

BEDROOMS

MSGSSS **Torres Alto Palermo** **Buenos Aires** **Argentina** Argentinien **1994**

Living in high-rise buildings has become a frequent solution for the upper middle-class in rapidly growing cities of the Southern hemisphere. In Buenos Aires, Argentina, the architectural firm MSGSSS (Manteola/Sanchez/Gomez/Santos/Solsona/Sallaberry Arquitectos) and its partners planned a number of outstanding up-market estates, among them Torres Alto Palermo (1994). Situated in a prestigious location, the two, thirty-five-storey towers contain spacious three to four bedroom apartments with a floor space of 300 to 350 square metres, a squash court, a gym and a sauna, their architectural design reflecting the luxurious character of the development. Other residential high-rise projects by MSGSSS include the Plaza Las Heras Towers, the five towers of the Nuevos Aires Complex and the seven tower blocks of the Rioja Housing Complex, the latter built for the employees of a large bank.

In den rasant wachsenden Städten der südlichen Halbkugel stellt das Wohnen im Hochhaus häufig eine Option für Besserverdienende dar, wie etwa in den Projekten der argentinischen Architekturfirma MSGSSS (Manteola/Sanchez Gomez/Santos/Solsona/ Sallaberry Arquitectos). Die elegante Architektur spiegelt den luxuriösen Charakter ihrer Wohntürme in **Buenos Aires**, wie zum Beispiel den 35-geschossigen **Torres Alto Palermo** (1994), wider.

WATERFRONT LIVING   WOHNEN AM WASSER

West 8
Borneo Island
Amsterdam   The Netherlands Niederlande   1996–2000

Designing new housing schemes in Amsterdam involves a double challenge: firstly, for almost a century, the Netherlands has had a pioneering role in setting new standards in social housing and new projects have to compete against the high architectural quality of existing estates; secondly, building land is scarce which results in high density urban areas. In the case of Amsterdam, brown-field development in parts of the old harbour may be the only realistic option for valuable building land near the city centre. This has led to a number of large-scale housing developments in recent years but few of them have actually reached the outstanding quality of the Borneo-Sporenburg area.

In 1996, the urban design and landscape architecture firm of West 8 was commissioned by the City of Amsterdam to work out a master plan to transform the two docks of Borneo and Sporenburg Islands into residential neighbourhoods with some 2,500 low-rise units. Together with sixty architects, West 8 developed a scheme which is clearly based on traditional Dutch small towns yet allows for a stunning variety of architectural forms. Strict, banded blocks follow the narrow shape of both peninsulas and are divided into small parcels – each 4.5–6×16 metres in size. Although designed by many different architects, all buildings follow a common typology based on the concept of the 'patio house' arranged around a private void while the larger blocks share a common courtyard. All patio residences are directly accessible from the narrow streets as well as from the waterfront, repeating the centuries-old model of Dutch canal houses. The result could be described as the highest possible diversity to be achieved within a uniform urban pattern. All individual dwellings have exactly the same height, and elements like garden doors were part of the urban brief. Nevertheless, the floor plans vary astonishingly as do the façades with their continuous change of dark and light brick elements or glass walls. The density is about 100 units per hectare.[1]

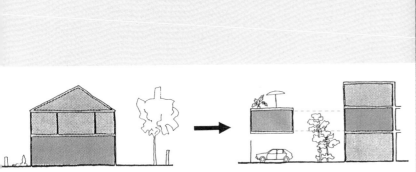

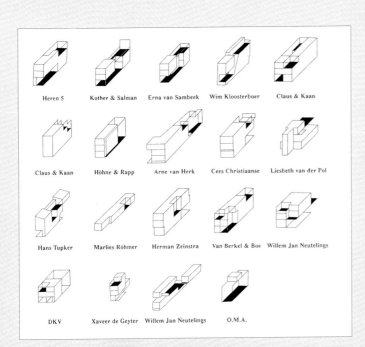

Heren 5	Kother & Salman	Erna van Sambeek	Wim Kloosterboer	Claus & Kaan
Claus & Kaan	Höhne & Rapp	Arne van Herk	Cees Christiaanse	Liesbeth van der Pol
Hans Tupker	Marlies Röhmer	Herman Zeinstra	Van Berkel & Bos	Willem Jan Neutelings
DKV	Xaveer de Geyter	Willem Jan Neutelings	O.M.A.	

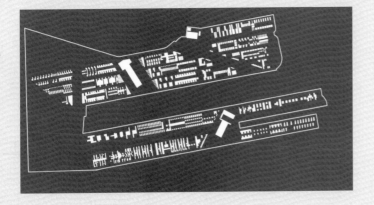

Among the architects involved in planning the small dwellings are MVRDV, OMA and Josep Lluís Mateo. The high-rise blocks include the impressive The Whale housing estate – also called the Sphinx – by de Architekten Cie. which has become one of Eastern Amsterdam harbour's landmarks. Its curved volume may appear artificial at first sight but in fact ensures that more sunshine reaches the inner courtyard.

West 8 also planned the public spaces which again aim at achieving a balance between traditional Dutch brick-paved streets and innovative architecture. Among the most beautiful elements are three bridges for pedestrians and cyclists of red painted steel and untreated timber connecting the two peninsulas. But it would not be the Netherlands if innovations were restricted purely to architectural vocabulary. Consequently the Borneo-Sporenburg project also experimented with creating a social mix within the new development. While dwellings range from exclusive apartments to social housing units, some sixty empty parcels were simply sold through the lottery and the future landlords and their architects were briefed by the developers – maybe a prototype for a new planning strategy in the Netherlands.[2]

1   Architectural Design, 2003, p. 14
2   ArchNewsNow, 2002

de Architekten Cie.   The Whale   Amsterdam   The Netherlands Niederlande   **1998–2000**

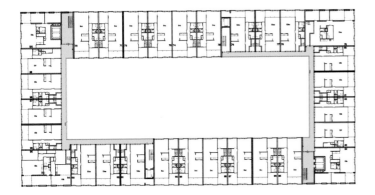

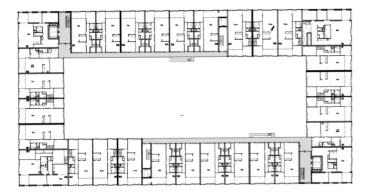

Die selbst für niederländische Maßstäbe außergewöhnliche Qualität der Wohngebiete Borneo und Sporenburg im Amsterdamer Hafen geht auf den Entwurf der Stadt- und Landschaftsplaner West 8 zurück. Zusammen mit 60 Architekten schufen sie ein auf traditionellen holländischen Stadtmodellen aufbauendes Bebauungsschema, das eine erstaunliche Bandbreite architektonischer Ausdrucksformen erlaubt. Am auffallendsten sind die um einen kleinen privaten Innenhof angeordneten Patio-Häuser auf einer Grundfläche von 4,5–6 mal 16 Metern mit direktem Zugang zum Wasser. Die Höhe ist einheitlich, die Fassaden dagegen sind völlig unterschiedlich – von lokaltypischen Ziegelmauern bis zu Vollverglasungen. Unter den Architekten sind MVRDV, OMA und Josep Lluís Mateo.

Ergänzt wird die niedrige Bebauung durch einzelne spektakuläre Hochbauten, darunter der beeindruckende Wohnblock **The Whale** von **de Architekten Cie.**, dessen auffällig gebogene Dachform eine optimale Belichtung der Wohnungen ermöglicht. West 8 sind auch für die sorgfältige Gestaltung aller Außenräume mit ihren schönen Brücken verantwortlich. Beachtlich ist die soziale Durchmischung in den neuen Wohngebieten – von Luxushäusern bis zu Sozialwohnungen.

Hans Kollhoff Piräus-Block KNSM Island, Amsterdam The Netherlands Niederlande **1994**

Recent years have witnessed new waterfront developments all over the world, primarily due to brown-field development strategies following the decline of traditional harbour industries. At the same time these projects reflect the search for more individualistic solutions to housing in an urban context. Not all of them involve housing, however, and results are quite diverse when it comes to architectural and environmental qualities. In the Netherlands, the residential building Piraeus on KNSM Island in Amsterdam, planned by the German architect Hans Kollhoff, offers an interesting counterpart to the Borneo-Sporenburg development. Kollhoff reacted to the rather rough and open harbour landscape by placing a massive yet carefully designed block, 170 x 60 metres, right on the edge of the waterfront. Contrasting surprisingly with the austere façades, the building respects both the natural and built surroundings. For example, the composition of the new buildings integrates an old house in the south and a public park in the west, opening the block up with a generous arcade. Living rooms are oriented to the south while the floor plans themselves are extremely flexible leading to almost 150 different types of dwelling.[3] The expressive zinc-capped sloped roof now serves as a landmark for the harbour area.

Einen interessanten Gegensatz zu Borneo-Sporenburg bildet die **KNSM-Insel** mit dem Wohnkomplex **Piräus** von **Hans Kollhoff**, der zu einem Wahrzeichen der neuen Hafenfront wurde. Von außen fast abweisend, reagiert er dennoch sensibel auf seine Umgebung und weist nicht weniger als 150 verschiedene Wohnungsgrundrisse auf.

Cesar Pelli   Solaire Apartments   Battery Park City, New York   USA   2000–2001

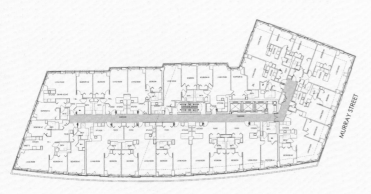

RIVER TERRACE

Lower Manhattan's waterfront has undergone dramatic changes in the last decades, including striking, new, up-market, housing projects. Among these, the Solaire Apartments at Battery Park City (the centre building closest to the shore pictured above) by Cesar Pelli (2000–01) are unique. The twenty-seven-storey, 252-unit, glass-and-brick residential tower, built entirely on a landfill, is based on strict environmental guidelines reducing energy consumption by at least thirty-five percent through a variety of technical innovations. Overlooking the harbour and the Statue of Liberty its elegant structure is to become an integral part of the Hudson waterfront respecting the scale of Pelli's earlier World Financial Center.

Zu den interessantesten neuen Wohnungsbauten am Wasser gehören die **Solaire Apartments** (Cesar Pelli, 2000/01) in Lower Manhattan, **New York**, mit einem innovativen Energiekonzept.

Foster & Partners   Albion Riverside   London   Great Britain Großbritannien   2003–2004

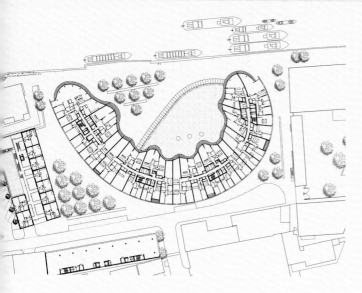

The Albion Riverside Development by Norman Foster (2003–04) occupies an equally prestigious location in central London. Situated right on the River Thames between Battersea Bridge and Albert Bridge it offers dramatic views over Westminster from each of its 183 apartments and thirteen duplex penthouses. It also includes a number of offices, restaurants and an indoor pool. Foster designed the building as a semicircular volume opening to the river. Façades are elegant, glass-aluminium structures underlining the high-tech planning approach as well as the luxurious aspects of this top-of-the-market residence.

Ironically, another high-tech residential building has been built in London, though under very different local circumstances. Grand Union Walk, designed by Nicholas Grimshaw back in 1986 on the site of a former industrial bakery, in the far less prestigious eastern borough of Camden Town, faces the Grand Union Canal to the north and busy Camden Road to the south. Thus Grimshaw decided to orient the apartments to the north, but a highly sophisticated system of automatically operated openings and electronically controlled aluminium elements [4] allows daylight to enter all rooms. Apartments vary from duplex units to maisonettes and studios. The long front along the canal is accentuated by alternately closed and open elements and a technical, almost sci-fi exterior is achieved by concrete blocks and aluminium panels connecting the façades with the roof. Grimshaw's work may seem extreme yet, at the same time, it offers a reasonable solution for high-standard, residential use under seemingly unfavourable conditions.

3   Oosterman, 1996, p. 107
4   Ravetllat, 1992, p. 167

144

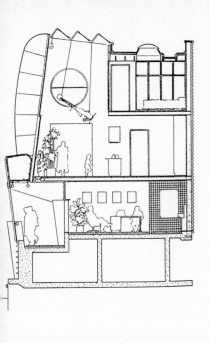

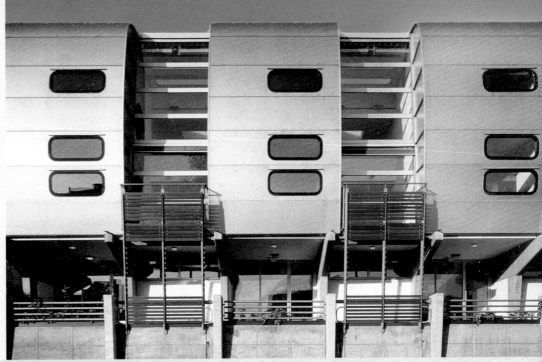

Nicholas Grimshaw Grand Union Walk London Great Britain Großbritannien 1986–1988

Massimiliano Fuksas Alsterfleet Housing Hamburg Germany Deutschland 1998–2002

There is some similarity between how a long and potentially monotonous block along a canal is structured, as at Grand Union Walk and the Alsterfleet Housing Development in Hamburg by Massimiliano Fuksas (1998–2002). In the latter, the block is broken up into individual towers, interrupted by gaps which give pedestrians access to the Alster path. The flexible floor plans allow one to five-roomed flats both for the open-market and the social housing sector. While the red brick surfaces of the supporting walls pick up on a traditional Nordic element, the fronts facing the Alster canal are completely open with glass walls. The daily comings and goings around the harbour, so closely connected with the image of Hamburg, have thus been newly interpreted in a very convincing way.

In London ist die direkt an der Themse gelegene luxuriöse Wohnanlage Albion Riverside von Norman Foster (2003/04) mit ihrer eleganten Glas-Aluminium-Fassade erwähnenswert; ebenso der von Nicholas Grimshaw bereits 1986 in einer viel weniger prestigeträchtigen Lage geplante Grand Union Walk: High-Tech-Architektur mit elektronisch gesteuerten beweglichen Aluminiumelementen, deren Rhythmus die lange Fassade am Kanal gliedert.

In ähnlicher Weise bricht Massimiliano Fuksas den langen Block der Wohnhäuser am Alsterfleet in Hamburg (1998–2002) auf: Turmartige Bauten wechseln mit öffentlichen Zugängen zur Alster. Während die Wände zwischen den Häusern die traditionelle Ziegelarchitektur Hamburgs aufnehmen, öffnen sich die Wohnungen mit großen Verglasungen zum Hafen.

SUSTAINABLE HOUSING   NACHHALTIGER WOHNUNGSBAU

Baumschlager & Eberle
Lohbach Residences Wohnbebauung am Lohbach
Innsbruck   Austria Österreich   2000

The Lohbach estate by the architects Carlo Baumschlager and Dietmar Eberle, who have been at the forefront of ecological innovation in housing for many years, resulted from a competition held by a non-profit, Tyrolean developer. It is situated in a peripheral yet densely built-up area of Innsbruck with a mix of low-rise and multi-storey residential buildings. The estate consists of six blocks of five to seven storeys, one of them with flats adapted for special needs and a care-centre for elderly residents. Aiming at economical and ecological optimisation, the compact volumes of the cube-like structures reduce the external wall area and have central staircases in covered inner courtyards. Ecological measures include solar energy panels, heat recovery plants and rain water use, emphasizing the cheap, low-tech solutions available for social housing schemes.

The tranquil general impression is underlined by the repetitive design of the façades. The blocks have double façades, the actual exterior walls being of painted timber elements, with an additional outer wrapper of foldable copper elements. This provides the apartments with a projecting balcony zone that can be opened or closed off completely, the variable composition of the shutters changing the building's appearance according to the time of day, the season or the residents' habits. Balcony sills are of frosted glass and when the shutters are folded back at the corners the buildings become surprisingly transparent, offering beautiful views both from inside and outside of the surrounding mountains. The buildings rest on pilotis; thus the ground floor steps back contributing to a lively interaction between built volumes and open areas and between private and public spaces.

Baumschlager & Eberle planned a number of similar housing estates across Europe. Though different in the use of material and always clearly responding to their specific locations, the projects are all characterized by ecological optimisation, by the use of few materials and by cost reduction through intelligent construction. These all combine to guarantee affordability in the provision of high-standard housing to low and middle-income households.

Carlo Baumschlager und Dietmar Eberle, seit Jahren Pioniere des ökologischen Wohnungsbaus, gewannen den von einem gemeinnützigen Tiroler Bauträger ausgelobten Wettbewerb am Stadtrand von Innsbruck. Die kostenmäßige und ökologische Optimierung führte zu kubischen fünf- bis siebengeschossigen Baukörpern mit möglichst geringen Außenflächen und innenliegendem, natürlich belichtetem Treppenhaus. Einer der sechs Blöcke beherbergt betreute Altenwohnungen. Zu den Low-Tech-Maßnahmen gehören Solarpaneele, Wärmerückgewinnung und Regenwassernutzung. Die Fassaden sind zweischalig – bestehend aus der holzverschalten Außenwand sowie aus Kupferläden, die den Balkonen vorgesetzt sind und komplett geöffnet oder geschlossen werden können. Je nach Tageszeit, Jahreszeit und Bewohnerverhalten ändert sich damit das äußere Erscheinungsbild der Anlage. Transparenz und Beziehung zur Umgebung – mit prachtvollen Ausblicken auf die umgebenden Bergketten – werden durch die zurückgesetzten Erdgeschosse und Balkonbrüstungen aus Mattglas unterstützt. In einer Reihe ähnlicher, jedoch immer auf die spezifische lokale Situation reagierender Wohnhausanlagen entwickelten die Architekten ihre Prinzipien der ökologischen Optimierung, der Reduzierung auf wenige Materialien und der Kostenminimierung durch intelligente Bauweisen weiter. Auch Haushalten mit niedrigerem Einkommen soll damit ein hoher Wohnungsstandard geboten werden.

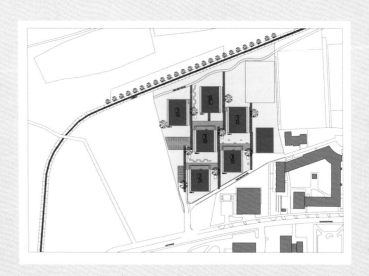

Shigeru Ban Hanegi Forest Tokyo Japan 1997

Environmental concerns have increasingly led to innovative solutions in urban housing all over the world. In a quiet residential area of Tokyo the very unusual Hanegi Forest estate by Shigeru Ban (1997) was based on the priority given to the preservation of twenty-seven large trees.[1] The steel frame construction follows a triangular grid of four metres providing free spatial composition in spite of a restricted budget. It allows small, circular and oval interior courtyards around the trees which give each of the eleven apartments – in fact three-storey terraced houses – a unique character. The elegant apartments seem to flow around the glassed voids. The building rests on pilotis, making the ground floor transparent and enhancing the sensation of a forest. In its careful detailing the building connects the simplicity of traditional Japanese architecture to the use of industrialized construction systems.

1   Broto, 2004, p. 172

Weltweit führt die Sorge um die Umwelt zu innovativen Lösungen im Wohnungsbau. Für das Wohnhaus Hanegi Forest in Tokyo (1997), bei dem 27 große Bäume erhalten werden mussten, entwickelte Shigeru Ban eine Stahlrahmenkonstruktion auf einem dreieckigen Raster, der trotz des beschränkten Budgets eine freie räumliche Komposition erlaubt. Durch kreisrunde oder ovale Öffnungen um die Bäume erhält jede der elf eleganten Wohnungen einen eigenen Charakter, und das transparente Erdgeschoss mit Pilotis verstärkt den Eindruck eines Waldes. Die sorgfältig geplanten Details verbinden die Einfachheit der traditionellen japanischen Architektur mit der Anwendung industrialisierter Bausysteme.

URBAN IMPLANTS　STÄDTISCHE IMPLANTATE

Philippe Gazeau
Housing Rue de l'Ourcq　Wohnhaus Rue de l'Ourcq
Paris　France　Frankreich　1990–1993

With housing in Paris being among the most expensive in Europe, the French Mail decided to build dwellings for young postmen arriving to work in the capital. Most of the new flats were designed as studios for single occupancy or small one-bedroom apartments. When Philippe Gazeau was commissioned with plans for such an estate at Rue de l'Ourcq in the densely built-up 19th arrondissement he was confronted with a narrow strip of land squeezed into a block of late 19th-century apartment buildings of nondescript style. The usual solution would have been to close the block by adding another building with apartments facing the street or the courtyard. Gazeau, however, presented an interesting alternative by slicing the building in two. As a result there are now two narrow wings stretching from the street into about half of the block one 3.5 metres wide and fifteen metres long, the other one 7.5 metres wide and in fact again cut in two. Thus the whole building is arranged around a void which, in turn, interlinks with the adjoining courtyards. This empty space includes the open staircase which protrudes at the back of the building and also serves as a communication area for the residents.

The design of the flats was treated with the utmost attention to detail. In spite of the limited space all of the flats receive a generous amount of natural light and most of them have access to balconies or terraces. The materials were equally carefully chosen, with elements in black brick, aluminium, glass and wood. The façade facing the street is characterized by floor-to-ceiling 'French' windows with sliding aluminium panels which provide privacy and, at the same time, create a lively pattern changing with the time of the day and with the habits of the tenants. Gazeau's work proves that low-cost housing need not look poor and that, despite the extreme density, a new building can improve the visual and spatial qualities of an area. Indeed, the situation from the street has clearly improved, with the building stepped back, creating additional space for a café. But it is, first of all, its sculptural effect and the skilful play with open and closed volumes that introduce a new relationship between public and private spaces.

Wohnungen in Paris gehören zu den teuersten in Europa, weshalb die französische Post den Bau von Kleinwohnungen für junge Postbedienstete beschloss. Philippe Gazeau wurde mit der Planung auf einem schmalen Grundstück in der Rue de l'Ourcq im dicht bebauten 19. Bezirk beauftragt. Abweichend vom üblichen Schema schloss er die Baulücke nicht vollständig, sondern teilte das Gebäude in zwei langgestreckte Trakte. Diese werden durch einen Freiraum verbunden, in dem das Treppenhaus als gemeinsamer Kommunikationsbereich liegt. Trotz des knappen Raums werden alle Wohnungen großzügig mit Tageslicht versorgt und verfügen über Zugang zu Balkonen oder Terrassen. Die Materialien wurden sorgfältig ausgewählt. Die Straßenfassade verfügt über französische Fenster mit verschiebbaren Aluminiumelementen und verändert sich daher im Tagesablauf und mit den Gewohnheiten der Bewohner. Gazeaus Arbeit zeigt, dass sozialer Wohnungsbau nicht billig aussehen muss, aber auch, dass die Implantierung eines neuen Gebäudes einem Gebiet selbst bei extremer Dichte neue visuelle und räumliche Qualitäten verleihen kann. Vor allem aber erzeugt das geschickte Spiel mit offenen und geschlossenen Baukörpern eine neue Beziehung zwischen öffentlichen und privaten Räumen.

RUE DE L'OURCQ

RUE DE NANTES

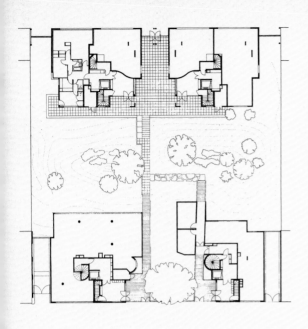

Christian de Portzamparc   Parc de Bercy   Paris   France Frankreich   1994

Among the French architects who have repeatedly dealt with the challenge of implanting new buildings into the complex fabric of Paris is Christian de Portzamparc. He participated in the huge development at Parc de Bercy in Paris. Its chief planner, Jean-Pierre Buffi, had laid down a number of principles to be followed by all architects: homogeneity in the overall forms, the use of the same materials (white stone and black painted aluminium) and gaps to visually relate the buildings to the park. Portzamparc's residential estate at Rue de l'Ambroise (1994) features a design approach similar to Gazeau's apartments for postal employees. Various building parts are visually unified by long strips of balconies on every second level while the duplex penthouses resemble small villas. Closed and open spaces, and public and private areas interconnect, creating a continuous dialogue between the architecture of the park and the surrounding buildings – both characterized by an unusually careful treatment of the surfaces.

Mit einem ähnlichen Ansatz folgt Christian de Portzamparc bei seinem Wohnhaus in der Rue de l'Ambroise am Parc de Bercy in Paris (1994) den verbindlichen Planungsvorgaben des Chefarchitekten Jean-Pierre Buffi – äußere Einheitlichkeit, gleiche Materialien, offene Bereiche zur optischen Verbindung von Gebäuden und Park. Geschlossene und offene Räume, öffentliche und private Bereiche durchdringen einander und schaffen einen Dialog zwischen der außergewöhnlichen Architektur des neuen Parks und jener der umgebenden Wohnbebauung.

THE FUTURE OF HOUSING IN THE 21ST CENTURY

At the beginning of the 21st century, for the first time ever, more than half of the world's population live in cities. There is, however, still a great difference between the industrialized countries (where more than seventy-two per cent of all residents live in cities) and the developing world (with thirty-seven per cent). In 2050 about eighty per cent worldwide are expected to be living in urban areas.[1] At the same time, the scale of urban agglomerations is dramatically changing: 'mega-cities', comprising urban cores and associated hinterlands, lead to a new quality of quantities. There are at present twenty-seven mega-cities of more than five million inhabitants of which eighteen are in Asia – five in India (Mumbai with fifteen million in 1995 and more than twenty-seven expected in 2015, Calcutta, Delhi, Hyderabad, Lahore) and three in China.[2] Each week, the world's urban population grows by one million. While it seems clear that this urbanization process cannot be stopped, it has led to completely new challenges concerning infrastructure, environment, governance and social fragmentation. The scale of the problem becomes even clearer when looking at the distribution of social groups within such mega-cities. In Mumbai, for example, fifty per cent of the population live in slums but occupy only eight per cent of the built-up area; similarly, in São Paulo more than half of the city's twenty-six million are squeezed into *favelas* and the infamous *corticos*. Thus, slums are characterized both by inappropriate services and extreme density. This chapter presents three possible answers to the challenges of urban hypergrowth:

Beijing, among the fastest growing cities in Asia, has been relying on continuous, yet planned growth. The enormous building programme has led to the demolition of most of the capital's historic residential areas which have been replaced by a seemingly endless, uniform grid of monotonous tower blocks. Housing focuses on the needs of those who have recently come into money and imitates European or American models. There are remarkable exceptions, though, including the fascinating project by Zaha Hadid which intends to replace final planning solutions by a 'fluid city' scheme based on a polycentric metropolitan concept. Other developments are intended to create an identity within this mega-city in the form of gated communities, or address the urgent problem of environmental pollution through the inclusion of innovative technical solutions. Still, unlimited growth is clearly accepted.

European cities have been confronted with very different problems, including the privatisation of urban spaces in the context of neo-liberal urban policies. This has increased spatial segregation but also carries risks for the functioning of society

as such, as its development has always been closely connected to the ideal of open, 'democratic' spaces. Architects are now looking for new approaches to integrate public spaces in the overall planning of new housing areas. Some of the most exciting examples include the recent addition to the traditional workers' housing area in Mulhouse, France, based on the master plan by Jean Nouvel, as well as a number of new community-orientated housing schemes in Britain. In a very different way the phenomenon of 'shrinking cities' with decreasing densities – as in Russia and Eastern Germany – offers unexpected potential for a redefinition of urban space.

However, it is the Third World where the negative effects of spatial segregation and social exclusion are becoming more and more evident. For example, in many cases the poor cannot afford public transport – if existent at all – to the city centres and are thus excluded from access to services and jobs. The traditional method of slum-clearance and large public housing schemes failed dramatically under such circumstances, repeating the vicious circle of upgrading programmes and quickly established informal settlements. In Asia and in other parts of the developing world – such as the large cities of South America – new approaches have been sought. Slums or *favelas* are now seen less as the problem but as part of the solution. If slum-dwellers have been able to cope with the most unfavourable conditions without any help why not use their existing social networks and support self-organisation and self-managed improvement? This informal sector fosters more and more non-state housing initiatives as the successful 'sites-and-services' example of Aranya in India and similar grass-root developments in Africa and Australia show. At the same time, an emergence of a new localism in housing architecture can be observed, making use of traditional construction techniques and locally available materials. Such schemes also respond to cultural and to environmental challenges, and respect differences in lifestyle.

1   United Nations Human Settlements Programme, Habitat, 2001
    and 2003; also Lo, 1994 and 1998
2   Beckel, 2001, p. 18

Am Anfang des 21. Jahrhunderts lebt erstmals mehr als die Hälfte der Weltbevölkerung in Städten. Im Jahr 2050 werden es 80 Prozent sein, doch der Anteil ist in den Industrieländern (72,6 Prozent) noch deutlich höher als in den Entwicklungsländern (37 Prozent). Von den 27 Megastädten mit mehr als fünf Millionen Einwohnern befinden sich 18 in Asien, davon fünf in Indien und drei in China. Jede Woche wächst die urbane Bevölkerung weltweit um eine Mil-

DIE ZUKUNFT DES WOHNENS IM 21. JAHRHUNDERT

lion. Dieser vermutlich nicht aufhaltbare Verstädterungsprozess führt zu völlig neuen Herausforderungen hinsichtlich Infrastruktur, Umwelt, Verwaltung und sozialer Fragmentierung. In Städten wie Mumbai und São Paulo lebt mehr als die Hälfte der Bevölkerung in Slums, die nicht nur eine mangelnde Infrastruktur aufweisen, sondern auch extreme Dichten. Dieses Kapitel stellt drei mögliche Antworten auf die Herausforderungen des Städtewachstums vor.

Peking etwa setzt nach wie vor auf unbegrenztes, wenn auch geplantes Wachstum. Das enorme Bauprogramm hat zur Zerstörung der meisten alten Wohnquartiere und zum Entstehen einer scheinbar endlosen uniformen Rasterstadt geführt, deren Wohnbauten europäische und amerikanische Vorbilder imitieren. Zu den bemerkenswerten Ausnahmen gehört Zaha Hadids Fluid City, deren Konzept einer polyzentrischen Stadtentwicklung anstelle endgültiger Planungslösungen folgt. Andere Wohnungsbauten zielen auf Identität in der Megastadt in Form von Gated Communities oder begegnen den dringenden Umweltproblemen mit neuen technischen Lösungen. Das Wachstum selbst wird nicht hinterfragt.

Europäische Städte sehen sich mit anderen Herausforderungen konfrontiert. So hat die neoliberale Planungsphilosophie zunehmend zu einer Privatisierung des öffentlichen Raums geführt – eine Gefahr für eine Gesellschaft, deren Entwicklung schon immer stark an allgemein zugängliche, ›demokratische‹ Räume gebunden war. In neuen Wohngebieten wie der Erweiterung der alten Arbeitersiedlung in Mulhouse, Frankreich, und in zahlreichen britischen Planungen wird daher versucht, neue Ansätze zu entwickeln, mit denen der öffentliche Raum in die Gesamtplanung integriert werden kann. Unerwartete Möglichkeiten für eine Neuinterpretation öffentlicher Räume schafft auch das verbreitete Phänomen der ›schrumpfenden Städte‹, wie etwa in Russland und Ostdeutschland.

Doch sind es die Städte der Dritten Welt, die immer deutlicher die negativen Auswirkungen räumlicher Segregation und sozialer Ausschließung zeigen. Vor allem in Asien und Südamerika wird daher zunehmend nach neuen Lösungen gesucht. Slums oder Favelas werden dabei nicht mehr als das eigentliche Problem, sondern als Beitrag zu einer Problemlösung verstanden, bei der bestehende soziale Netze und die Selbstorganisation der Bewohner im Vordergrund stehen. Dies führt zu erfolgreichen Projekten wie in Aranya, Indien, und ähnlichen Beispielen in Afrika und Australien. Gleichzeitig macht sich eine neue, an traditionellen Bautechniken und lokal verfügbaren Materialien orientierte Wohnarchitektur bemerkbar, die auf kulturelle Veränderungen, Umweltprobleme und verschiedenartige Lebensstile reagiert.

UNLIMITED GROWTH   UNBEGRENZTES WACHSTUM

Zaha Hadid Architects
Soho City
Beijing Peking   China   2004

With a population of more than 1.3 thousand million, China is to-day the fourth largest economy in the world with a continuous growth and an uninterrupted influx to its urban areas. This has resulted in an enormous growth of the big cities involving large-scale demolition of – often culturally valuable – inner city districts, and to a construction programme practically unrivalled by any other country. Beijing, of course, is one of the hubs of this development which is further enhanced by the 2008 Olympic Games. As Chinese politicians are eager to attract international know-how in the field of planning, the list of foreign architects involved in the Olympic projects reads like the 'Who-is-Who' of world architecture, with Herzog & de Meuron, Paul Andreu, Ove Arup, Rem Koolhaas and others forming partnerships with Chinese firms.

While commissions for most of the prestigious public buildings have been given to such star architects, housing has mostly been left to standardized and rather repetitive developments of

disputable quality – often simply imitating European or American architectural models – replacing the traditional, low-rise, inner city areas with monotonous tower blocks. Mostly they are clearly directed at an affluent, nouveau-riche clientele. This has led to a patchwork of urban dormitories rather than to a liveable metropolis. Only recently has good architecture been discovered as a selling point, and a number of foreign architects have been participating in competitions for new housing estates. Among them, the Soho City project by Zaha Hadid is the most noteworthy.

Commissioned by Sohochina,[1] a successful developer founded in 1995, Zaha Hadid deliberately breaks up the dominant grid pattern planning scheme of the Chinese capital. The envisaged development in the south-east of Beijing follows the concept of a 'fluid city' which abolishes the search for final planning solutions. Instead, Hadid introduces the idea of a polycentric metropolis by offering a new kind of geometry of converging

lines, open to contextual adaptations and supporting a functional mix. The new name of the area thus stands both for the developing company and for the energetic vitality of SoHo in Manhattan.

A common focus animates the building mass which is neither randomly scattered nor dictated by Beijing's monotonous grid. Instead, Hadid intends to offer a development model which provides both moments of intimacy and of identity within an endlessly expanding mega-city.

Generating unity from diversity is the aim of the ambitious project[2] – which could serve as a flexible model for other large urbanized areas.

1 Architektur aktuell, 2004, p. 110
2 Hadid, 2005

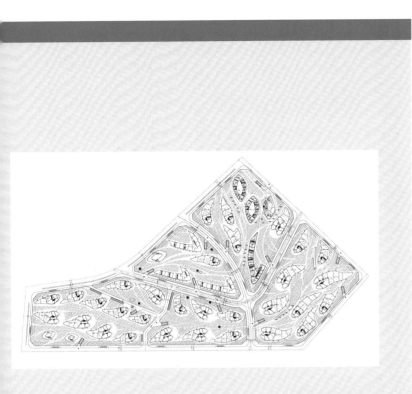

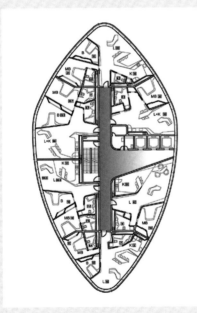

Der Wirtschaftsboom in China, mit 1,3 Milliarden Einwohnern bereits die viertgrößte Wirtschaftsmacht der Welt, führt zu einem weltweit kaum vergleichbaren Zustrom in die Städte und zum großflächigen Abbruch von – oft kulturhistorisch wertvollen – innerstädtischen Gebieten. Peking, zudem mit den Planungen für die Olympischen Spiele 2008 befasst, ist natürlich ein Zentrum dieser Entwicklung. Zu den Architekten, die derzeit in der chinesischen Hauptstadt planen, gehören internationale Stars wie Herzog & de Meuron, Paul Andreu, Ove Arup und Rem Koolhaas, meist in Partnerschaft mit chinesischen Büros.

Im Gegensatz zu den spektakulären öffentlichen Gebäuden bleibt ein Großteil der neuen Wohnprojekte architektonisch anspruchslos und monoton, oft einfach Imitate europäischer oder amerikanischer Vorbilder für eine zahlungskräftige Mittelschicht. Zu den wenigen Ausnahmen gehört Soho City von Zaha Hadid, die den uniformen Blockraster Pekings durch eine ›fließende‹, zukünftigen Entwicklungen offenstehende Stadt aufbrechen will. Ihre Geometrie konvergierender Linien beruht auf dem Konzept einer polyzentrischen Metropole. Soho steht daher nicht nur für den Namen des Bauträgers (Sohochina), sondern auch für die urbane Vielfalt und Anpassungsfähigkeit des gleichnamigen Stadtteils in New York. In der endlosen Megacity Peking sollen Intimität und Identität ermöglicht und Einheit in der Verschiedenheit geschaffen werden – ein Modell, das auch für andere urbane Agglomerationen anwendbar sein könnte.

OVERALL ELEVATION WEST

Steven Holl Architects   Looped Hybrid   Beijing Peking   China   2004–2006

Steven Holl experiments in a different way with the position of residential skyscrapers in the Looped Hybrid (2004–06) complex with
700 apartments situated adjacent to the old city walls of Beijing.
Instead of extending the monotonous city development with even
more free standing towers this project aims primarily at creating
an urban space. The eight towers are linked on the twentieth floor
by a sky loop containing cafes and services for the 2,500 residents;
this is complemented by a public base loop for a number of different uses. It encircles a semi-public park with special recreational
areas or 'mounds'[3] for children, youths, middle-aged residents
and the elderly. Apartments offer girderless ceilings and views in
at least two directions.

Holl also employs special polychromatic schemes inspired
by the traditional architecture of China, providing a dramatic impression at night. Coloured membranes are used as well as mist-
ing fountains, while the integrated Cineplex will project images of
ongoing films onto sections of buildings and across water basins.
Holl's approach may be interpreted as creating an identity within
this mega-city – or, as a very special expression of up-market living
in a kind of gated community: almost the opposite of Zaha Hadid's
'fluid city'.

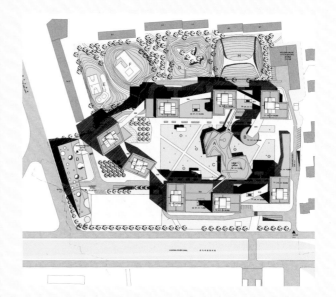

Steven Holl sucht im Wohnprojekt Looped Hybrid (2004–2006)
einen völlig anderen Zugang zum Thema Wohnen in der Megacity.
Acht Türme umgeben einen halböffentlichen Park mit abgegrenz-
ten Freizeitbereichen für unterschiedliche Benutzergruppen, während ein Skywalk mit Cafés und anderen Einrichtungen die Türme
verbindet. Holls Konzept gleicht aber eher einer Gated Community als Hadids offenem Stadtmodell.

Baumschlager & Eberle   MOMA Apartments   Beijing Peking   China   2004–2006

Another high-rise residential estate in China is being planned by the Austrian architectural firm of Baumschlager & Eberle. Having been involved in a number of environmentally orientated – though much smaller – housing projects all over Europe, they won a competition for a new housing estate at one of Beijing's busiest traffic hubs. Consequently, building services constitute an integral aspect of the MOMA Apartments (2004–06) and may be seen as a contribution to solving China's increasing environmental problems. Special attention was given to the latest sustainable technologies[4] including self-regulating façades with automatic ventilation. Apartments are generally larger taking into account traditional multi-generation households as well as the purchasing power of a growing number of moneyed city residents while the architectural repertoire remains deliberately European to fulfil current consumer demands.[5] The up-market character of the estate is further underlined by the choice of materials, like copper panels on the façades and black stone in the elegant lobbies. The five towers, with heights varying from eighty to 100 metres, are connected by a lower building, part comprising offices and shops. The total usable floor area is 100,000 square metres, adding considerable density at the edge of the inner city.

3   www.arcspace.com, 2004
4   www.baumschlager-eberle.com, 2004
5   Architektur aktuell, 2004, pp. 2–3

Ein weiterer Gesichtspunkt wird vom für seine ökologisch optimierten Wohnbauten bekannten österreichischen Architekturbüro **Baumschlager & Eberle** in den **MOMA Apartments** (2004–2006) eingebracht. Die fünf Türme im Zentrum Pekings verfügen unter anderem über selbstregulierende Fassaden mit automatischer Belüftung. Anspruchsvolles Wohnen soll – trotz wachsender Umweltprobleme – auch in zentralen Lagen möglich sein.

SPACES FOR AN OPEN SOCIETY   RÄUME FÜR EINE OFFENE GESELLSCHAF

Duncan Lewis/Scape Architecture + Block, Lacaton & Vassal
La Cité Manifeste
Mulhouse   France Frankreich   2003

In the Alsatian industrial town of Mulhouse, the Cité Ouvrière marked the beginning of French, 19th-century social housing. This pioneering estate of 1,240 terraced workers' houses was built with state subsidies by the newly founded Somco Association. Since then, it has undergone continuous alteration by the residents, reflecting their changing lifestyles and needs. To celebrate its 150th birthday, Somco once again decided to invest in innovative low-cost housing.[1] It invited Jean Nouvel to establish a team of – mostly younger – architects to provide plans for five large plots adjacent to the existing Cité. Other architects include Shigeru Ban and Matthieu Poitevin, with the most innovative solutions coming from Duncan Lewis in cooperation with the design group Scape Architecture + Block, and the office of Anne Lacaton & Jean-Philippe Vassal.

Lewis' design reflects the vernacular oddities and garden structures of the old social housing area but, at the same time, is a reminder of the 1960s utopian city structures. A supporting steel-tech system with high-grain plywood elements is complemented by vertical and horizontal mesh cages which provide the supports for blocks of vegetation between the houses and on the roofs. Living rooms are designed as five-metre cubes allowing the addition of interior galleries. The whole development is characterized by extreme flexibility both of closed and open spaces, intermingled with functional areas which can be adjusted to individual needs, as in the case of the old Cité Ouvrière. Lewis' concept, however, evolved from a very different design approach which instigates the exchange between totality and the fragmented, and between private and public space. It offers new possibilities but leaves it up to future residents to make use of them to create a new community.

The row of narrow terrace houses planned by Lacaton & Vassal consists of pre-fabricated concrete elements on the ground floor and an open steel structure above. This skeleton is filled with transparent poly-carbonate walls like conservatories which, unfortunately, caused severe heat insulation problems. The dwellings are to be seen as empty boxes which can be divided individually with all houses having generous terraces, but retaining the traditional separation between the built block and public street.

1   see Robert, 2005, pp. 10–23

Developments by Lacaton & Vassal (above) and Duncan Lewis with Scape Architecture + Block (below)
Wohnhäuser von Lacaton & Vassal (oben) und Duncan Lewis mit Scape Architecture + Block (unten)

Die Cité Ouvrière im elsässischen Mulhouse markierte im frühen 19. Jahrhundert den Beginn des sozialen Wohnungsbaus in Frankreich und reflektiert in ihren vielfältigen Veränderungen den Wandel der Lebensstile und Bedürfnisse ihrer Bewohner. Der gemeinnützige Bauträger Somco lud anlässlich seines 150-jährigen Bestehens Jean Nouvel ein, ein Team meist jüngerer Architekten zur Erweiterung dieser Arbeitersiedlung zu nominieren – unter ihnen Shigeru Ban und Matthieu Poitevin. Die innovativsten Ansätze lieferten jedoch Duncan Lewis gemeinsam mit der Designgruppe Scape Architecture + Block und das Büro Anne Lacaton & Jean-Philippe Vassal. Lewis nimmt in seinen Bauten Details der –

oft sehr eigenwillig veränderten – alten Siedlungshäuser auf, knüpft mit dem tragenden Stahlgerüst aber auch an die utopischen Stadtmodelle der 1960er-Jahre an. Stahlkäfige dienen als Vegetationsstützen. Die gesamte Anlage zeichnet sich durch Flexibilität im Inneren und in den Außenräumen aus. Lewis thematisiert damit die vielfältigen Beziehungen zwischen der Gesamtform und ihren Teilen, zwischen privatem und öffentlichem Raum. Lacaton & Vassal hingegen setzen auf eine traditionelle Trennung von Gebäude und Straße. Ihre Wohnhäuser erinnern an Gewächshäuser und können nach Belieben unterteilt werden. Allerdings sind sie klimatechnisch nicht unproblematisch.

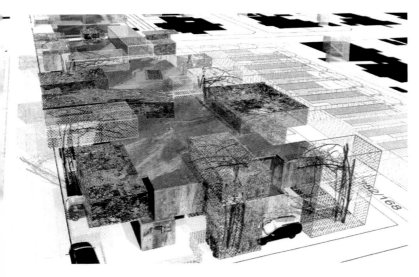

Proctor and Matthews   Abode   Newhall, Harlow   Great Britain Großbritannien   2004

In Britain, with its predominance of single-family terraced housing, new design approaches have been sought in order to overcome the privatisation-of-space policies of the Thatcher era. The government-supported creation of residential districts – to replace the vandalised post-war housing estates, on the one hand and the free-market gated community concept on the other – has led to the creation of a number of innovative estates with a renewed interest in the street and in public spaces. This includes traffic-calming measures but also influences the overall layout of such higher-density developments. The Abode green-field housing area at Newhall, Harlow by the architects Proctor and Matthews represents a strikingly fresh approach to urban community planning, its hierarchy of roads and paths focussing on the structure of external spaces to encourage community interaction. House entrances protrude into the street, giving it rhythm and enhancing the impression of a shared communal space, while verandas and screens mediate a level of privacy and openness which the architects describe as a 'framework for interaction'.[2]

Spaces for an open society and for new forms of housing can also be the consequence of decreasing densities. Given the world-wide increase in urban population this phenomenon of 'shrinking cities'[3] may seem surprising, but, in fact, the growth of certain urban areas has always been accompanied by the decline of others. Old industrialized centres or harbour areas like those found in Manchester or Liverpool may serve as examples of extreme stagnation after WW II and, if often rather euphemistical, of a later urban renaissance. Another prominent case is the city of Detroit, with probably the largest and most striking continual shrinking process due to social and racial conflicts and to unbroken suburbanisation. Today, there are actually more shrinking cities than boom towns; in the last fifty years most of them could be found in the USA (50) and in Great Britain (27) but in recent years the phenomenon has shifted to other parts of the world: to Russia and to former East Germany, for example.

In Russia, the city of Ivanovo illustrates the country's enormous economic and social turmoil. Once the centre of Soviet textile production, it has now lost most of its industry and the population is rapidly declining as young people, who can afford it, leave for other parts of Russia. A similar development can be seen in large parts of former East Germany, due to migration to western Germany, a falling birth-rate, and an increase in suburbanisation. Halle, for example, has lost some twenty per cent of its population since the early 1990s and Leipzig decreased from over 700,000 to 490,000 in the same period. Unoccupied dwellings in these cities amount to some twenty per cent, with large stretches of derelict housing lining the streets. Ironically, many of these pre-fabricated estates underwent heavily subsidised renovation after the reunification of Germany, while today state subsidies are being provided for their demolition. How should such a situation be dealt with properly? Intense discussion has focussed on the consequences of urban shrinkage and, today, it is generally accepted that this process is irreversible. It may even offer a chance to establish a new form of urban quality. The Büro für urbane Projekte presented their concept of a 'perforated city' which earmarks empty plots to be used for urban conversion aimed at low density housing. While, unfortunately, the suburbanisation process continues – with thousands of private houses built every year – the inner cities of eastern Germany have "involuntarily become large urban laboratories for a society in a state of change. Given their generous supply of space and their direct confrontation with reality they offer a surprising and unexpected potential."[4] Thus, the cycle of boom and decline need not necessarily follow the disastrous American city model which left urban development to the whim of the market economy,

Rückbau vorgesehenen Plattenbauten vorher mit staatlicher Förderung saniert wurden. Mittlerweile hat sich die Ansicht durchgesetzt, dass dieser Schrumpfungsprozess nicht umkehrbar ist; er kann aber Chancen für neue städtische Qualitäten eröffnen. Das vom **Büro für urbane Projekte** präsentierte Konzept der »perforierten Stadt« versteht die leerstehenden innerstädtischen Grundstücke als Ansatz zur Stadtumwandlung mit geringeren Dichten. Zwar geht der Prozess der Suburbanisierung weiter, doch werden die ostdeutschen Städte zunehmend zum Labor für eine Gesellschaft im Wandel. Der Kreislauf von Aufschwung und Niedergang muss nicht unbedingt dem verheerenden amerikanischen Stadtmodell folgen, das die Entwicklung der Städte dem Spiel der Marktkräfte überlässt und damit zu sozialer Segregation und zum Verfall ganzer Stadtteile führt. Er könnte stattdessen zur Schaffung eines sozialen und nachhaltigen städtischen Umfelds führen.

thus leading to social segregation and to the decline of complete urban districts. Instead the period of low economic development could be used to create a more cohesive and sustainable urban environment.

2   Wilson, 2003, p. 48
3   see the ongoing 'shrinking cities project': www.shrinkingcities.com
4   Käpplinger, 2005, p. 91

In Großbritannien versuchen zahlreiche neue Wohnsiedlungen, der Privatisierung des öffentlichen Raums während der Thatcher-Ära entgegen zu wirken. Anlagen wie **Abode** in **Newhall, Harlow** von den Architekten **Proctor and Matthews** entstehen im Zuge der von der Regierung geförderten Nachbarschaftsplanung. Die besonders sorgfältige Gestaltung öffentlicher und halböffentlicher Bereiche und ihrer Übergänge bietet den Rahmen für Kommunikation und Interaktion der Bewohner.

Auch eine Verringerung der Dichte kann zu Räumen für eine offene Gesellschaft führen, wie sich am Beispiel ›schrumpfenden Städte‹ zeigt. Zwar sind solche Entwicklungen nicht neu – man denke nur an den Niedergang alter Industrie- und Hafenstädte wie **Manchester, Liverpool** oder **Detroit**. Heute hat sich diese Entwicklung zu einem großen Teil in andere Regionen verlagert; schrumpfende Städte finden sich vor allem in Russland (etwa in **Ivanovo**, dem alten Zentrum der Textilindustrie) und Ostdeutschland. So hat **Halle** seit Anfang der 1990er-Jahre 20 Prozent seiner Einwohner verloren, und die Bevölkerung von **Leipzig** fiel von mehr als 700 000 auf 490 000. Der Wohnungsleerstand beträgt etwa 20 Prozent, wobei viele der nun zum geförderten Abbruch oder

Demolition of a prefabricated building Abbruch eines Plattenbaus   **Leipzig**   Germany Deutschland

BACK TO THE ROOTS ZURÜCK ZU DEN URSPRÜNGEN

Balkrishna Vithaldas Doshi
Aranya Community Housing Wohnsiedlung Aranya
Indore India Indien 1988–1995

For a long time India, like most emerging countries, has relied on urban development models imported from industrialized nations, such as slum clearance together with the construction of New Towns to help cope with the increase in population. In most cases, this has failed dramatically, as in the mega-city of Delhi, where six satellite towns and eleven peripheral 'priority towns' have, in fact, grown together, forming an immense urban agglomeration with thousands of informal settlements. With more people moving in, many of the more centrally located slum areas have become subject to land speculation and to upgrading programmes, driving the poorest to even more peripheral areas and repeating the vicious circle of planned growth and informal settlements. Sustainable solutions in housing depend, therefore, on the active involvement of the deprived and most vulnerable and a number of innovative solutions have been found and implemented in India.

Aranya, six kilometres from Indore, was planned by the Vastu-Shilpa Foundation under Balkrishna Vithaldas Doshi, a Le Corbusier co-operator at Chandigarh. Designed to house a total of 60,000, it aims at a mixture of different income groups, with the poorest allocated sixty-five per cent of the 6,500 plots mostly in the central parts of the different residential sectors. Upper-income plots were sold at profit to raise surplus capital and six acres were set aside to absorb the pockets of existing light industry. What makes the scheme a promising model, however, is the 'sites and services' approach for the low-cost units.[1] A fully serviced plot includes a basic building core – comprising toilet, washing facilities and electricity – which can be extended by the occupants at their own pace and with their own resources. Brick, stone and cement are available at a low price, with owners free to use any material of their choice – including clay – for further construction. While this has helped to make housing affordable to poor residents it has also succeeded in creating a fairly balanced community. Additionally, the overall design shows a closer regard for the traditional lifestyle of the people. Doshi planned some demonstration houses and insisted on a careful design of open spaces but basically it was the residents themselves who created a remarkably diverse architecture within a self-organising community. Acknowledging the model character of Aranya, Doshi received the Aga Khan Award for Architecture in 1995.

1 Doshi, 1988, p. 24

Step-by-step development from basic building cores to individual housing   Schrittweiser Ausbau der Hauskerne zu individuellen Wohnhäusern

Wie viele Entwicklungsländer hatte Indien zunächst Planungsansätze der Industrieländer übernommen, wie die Beseitigung von Slums und den Bau von New Towns. In den meisten Fällen scheiterten diese Planungen und führten zu einem Teufelskreis aus Stadtwachstum und neuen Slums. Die Stadt Aranya bei Indore wurde von der Vastu Shilpa Foundation unter Balkrishna Vithaldas Doshi, dem Partner Le Corbusiers in Chandigarh, für 60 000 Einwohner geplant. 65 Prozent aller Baugründe wurden an die ärmsten Familien vergeben, das Ziel war aber eine sozial durchmischte Gemeinschaft. Das innovative Konzept sah den Bau von Hauskernen mit Sanitäranlage, Wasser- und Stromanschluss vor, der weitere Ausbau und die Materialwahl blieben den Bewohnern überlassen. Dies machte die Häuser auch für Arme erschwinglich, zugleich ist die bemerkenswert vielfältige Architektur weit entfernt von der üblichen Missachtung traditioneller Lebensstile. Doshi entwarf einige Musterhäuser sowie die öffentlichen Räume und erhielt für seine Planung 1995 den Aga-Khan-Architekturpreis. Ähnliche Ansätze verfolgt das 1985 mit dem Right Livelihood Award, dem ›alternativen Nobelpreis‹ ausgezeichnete **Lokayan-Projekt** von **Rajendra Ravi**, das innovative Verkehrskonzepte mit neuen Stadtplanungsansätzen verbindet.

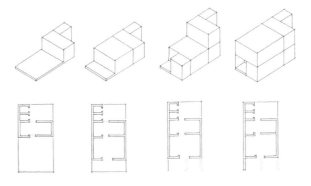

Hassan Fathi   New Gourna   Luxor   Egypt Ägypten   1946

Similarly, the Lokayan Project in India, founded by a group of scientists and planners under the leadership of Rajendra Ravi, aims at incorporating new transport concepts in plans for low-cost housing areas and involves the inclusion of vulnerable groups in the urban development process. Lokayan, today under the umbrella of the Delhi-based Institute for Democracy and Sustainability, has carried out a number of impressive projects and was honoured for its work with the Right Livelihood Award (the 'alternative Nobel Prize') in 1985.

The search for new housing concepts in the developing countries has not been limited to India, of course. Back in 1964 Bernard Rudofsky remarked that "architectural history, as written and taught in the Western world, has never been concerned with more than a few select cultures… with never a word about the houses of lesser people."[2] He suggested to "learn that many audacious 'primitive' solutions anticipate our cumbersome technology; that many a feature invented in recent years is old hat in vernacular architecture…"[3] Among the architects who pioneered low-cost housing based on local lifestyles was Hassan Fathi who became known across the globe as a result of his designs for the Egyptian villages of New Gourna and Bariz.[4] Fathi employed local building

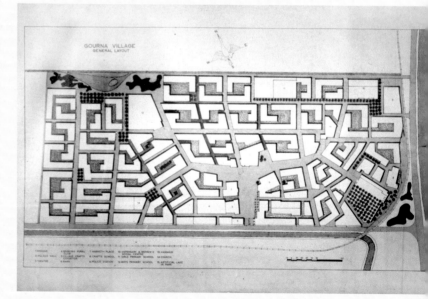

techniques and local materials like unbaked clay bricks. He was among the first to receive the Right Livelihood Award for his groundbreaking work in 1980.

In Australia, breaking the long history of inappropriate housing for Aboriginal communities, Troppo Architects designed the Galiwin'ku project on Arnhem Land in 1998. Their design was based on elaborate research and the analysis of indigenous kinship structures. Such schemes replace the former assimilation policy and reflect the new – if still scarce – recognition of Aboriginal culture as part of Australia's multicultural heritage. Housing design is based on living patterns at different times of the year, household structures, external orientation and the use of storage and resources, etc., as a response to cultural changes and to environmental challenges. Far beyond Aboriginal housing, this aims at a new understanding of changing lifestyles and at a housing-as-process philosophy[5] which may eventually lead to buildings which 'have their roots in the soil'.[6]

2 Rudofsky, 1977, p. 7
3 Rudofsky, 1977, p. 12
4 Fathi, 1969
5 Memmott, 2004
6 Doshi, 1987, p. 236

Die Suche nach neuen Wohnungsbaukonzepten für Entwicklungsländer beschränkt sich natürlich nicht auf Indien. Schon 1964 hatte Bernard Rudofsky die Architekturtheorie dafür kritisiert, dass sie sich ausschließlich mit wenigen ausgewählten Kulturen und praktisch nie mit der Wohnsituation der einfachen Leute beschäftigte. Sie sollte daher mehr von der Bautechnik der anonymen Architektur lernen. Unter den Pionieren einfacher und kostengünstiger Häuser ist Hassan Fathi, der mit seinen Lehmziegelbauten in den ägyptischen Dörfern New Gourna and Bariz weltbekannt wurde. Fathi war 1980 einer der ersten Preisträger des Right Livelihood Award. In Australien entwarfen Troppo Architects 1998 mit der Siedlung Galiwin'ku im Arnhem Land erstmals eine an den kulturellen Gewohnheiten und Bedürfnissen der Aboriginals orientierte Wohnungsanlage. In ihrem Verständnis unterschiedlicher Lebensstile und des prozessorientierten Wohnungsbaus gehen die Architekten weit über die Aboriginal-Frage hinaus auf die Suche nach Gebäuden, die – nach Doshi – »in der lokalen Erde wurzeln«.

BIBLIOGRAPHY BIBLIOGRAPHIE

General Allgemein

Alexander, Christopher (ed.), *A New Theory of Urban Design*, New York 1987

Allen, Judith et al., *Housing and Welfare in Southern Europe*, London 2005

Appleyard, Donald, *The Conservation of European Cities*, Cambridge MA 1979

Banham, Reyner, *Theory and Design in the First Machine Age*, London 1960

Barlow, Anne and Simon Duncan, *Success And Failure in Housing Provision, European Systems Compared*, Oxford 1994

Beckel, Lothar (ed.), *Mega Cities*, Salzburg 2001

Burt, Martha R., *Over the Edge, Growth of Homelessness in the 1980s*, New York 1992

Caldeira, Teresa, 'Fortified Enclaves, The New Urban Segregation' in Public Culture, no. 8, Durham 1996

Castells, Manuel, *The Informal City, Information Technology, Economic Restructuring and the Urban-Regional Process*, London 1989

Castells, Manuel, 'Grassrooting the Space of Flows' in Urban Geography, no. 20, Columbia 1999

Centre on Housing Rights and Evictions, The Human Right to Adequate Housing, A Chronology of United Nations Activity 1945–1999, Geneva 2000

Chapman, Michael and Alan Murie, 'Housing and the European Union' in Housing Studies, no. 11(2), Oxford 1996

Cocchioni, Cristina, Mario De Grassi, *La casa popolare a Roma*, Rome 1984

Conrads, Ulrich, *Programme und Manifeste zur Architektur des 20. Jahrhunderts*, Berlin/Frankfurt/Vienna 1964

Crowhurst Lennard, Susanne and Henry L. Lennard, *Public Life in Urban Places*, Southampton N.Y. 1984

Daly, Gerald, *Homeless, Policies, Strategies and Lives on the Street*, London 1996

Engels, Friedrich, *Zur Wohnungsfrage*, 1872 (transl.: *The Housing Question*, New York 1935)

Ewing, Reid, *Developing Successful New Communities*, Washington 1991

Farmer, Ben and Hentie Louw (eds.), *Companion to Contem-porary Architectural Thought*, London/New York 1993

FEANTSA, European Federation of National Organizations Working with the Homeless, *Europe Against Exclusion, Housing for All*, Brussels 1998

Fitch, J. M., *Architecture and the Esthetics of Plenty*, New York 1961

Förster, Wolfgang, 'Social Housing Design' in UNECE, 2005

Frampton, Kenneth, *Modern Architecture and the Critical Present*, London 1982

Friedman, Yona, *Structures Serving the Unpredictable*, Rotterdam 1999

Friedrichs, Jürgen, *Affordable Housing and the Homeless*, New York 1988

Garau, Pietro and Elliott D. Sciar (eds.), *A Home in the City. Improving the Lives of Slum Dwellers*, London 2005

Glazer, Nathan and Mark Lilla, *The Public Face of Architecture*, New York 1987

Häussermann, Hartmut and Walter Siebel, *Neue Urbanität*, Frankfurt 1987

Hitchcock, Henry-Russell et al., *The Rise of an American Architecture*, New York/Washington/London 1970

Jacobs, Jane, *The Death and Life of Great American Cities*, New York 1961

Joint Center for Housing Studies, *The State of the Nation's Housing*, 2000, Cambridge MA 2000

Krantz, B., E. Oresjo and Hugo Priemus, *Large Scale Housing in North West Europe, Problems, Interventions, Experiences*, Delft 1999

Kruft, Hanno-Walter, *A History of Archi-tectural Theory*, New York 1994

Le Bris, Émile, *Villes du Sud*, Paris 1996

LeGates, Richard T. and Frederic Stout, *The City Reader*, London/New York 1996

Leitmann, Josef, *Sustaining Cities, Environmental Planning and Manage-ment in Urban Design*, New York 1999

Lewin, AC, *Housing Co-operatives in Developing Countries, A Manual for Self-Help in Low-Cost Housing Schemes*, Chichester/New York 1981

Lo, Fu-Chen and You-Man Yeung (eds.), *Mega-City. Growth and Future*, Tokyo/New York/Paris 1994

Lo, Fu-Chen and You-Man Yeung (eds.), *Globalization and the World of Large Cities*, Tokyo/New York/Paris 1998

Mallgrave, Harry Francis, *Modern Architectural Theory. A Historical Survey*, Cambridge/New York 2005

Mitscherlich, Alexander, *Die Unwirtlichkeit unserer Städte*, Frankfurt 1965

Mollenkopf, John and Manuel Castells, *Dual City, Restructuring New York*, New York 1991

Mumford, Lewis, *The City in History. Its Origins, Its Transformations, and Its Prospects*, New York 1961

OECD, *Innovative Policies for Sustainable Urban Development, The Ecological City*, Paris 1996

Sassen, Saskia, *The Global City*, Princeton 1991

Sassen, Saskia, *Cities in a World Economy*, Thousand Oaks 1994

Scandinavian Housing and Planning Research, vol. 14, issues 1–4, Oslo/Oxford 1997/98

Short, John and Yeong-Hyun Kim, *Globalization and the City*, Harlow 1999

Simone, AbdouMaliq and Abdelghani Abouhani, *Urban Africa. Changing Customs of Survival in the City*, London/Dakar/Pretoria 2005

Towers, Graham, *An Introduction to Urban Housing Design*, Oxford 2005

UNECE-Committee on Human Settle-ments (ed.), *Guidelines on Social Housing*, Geneva 2005

United Nations Human Settlements Programme (ed.), *Cities in a Globalizing*

World, Global Report on Human Settlements, Nairobi/London 2001

United Nations Human Settlements Programme (ed.), The Challenge of Slums. Global Report on Human Settlements, Nairobi/London 2003

Van Vliet, Willem, Encyclopedia of Housing, Thousand Oaks 1998

Veltz, Pierre, Mondialisation, Villes et Territoires, Paris 1996

Weber, Max, Die Stadt, Tübingen 1914 (transl. The City, New York 1958)

Primary Sources **Primärliteratur**

Andersson, Magnus, Stockholm's Annual Rings, Stockholm 1997

Architectural Review, London, vol. October 1954

Architectural Review, London, no. 1252, June 2001

Architectural Design, London, vol. 73, no. 4, July/August 2003

Architektur aktuell, 7–8/2004, Vienna

Bauausstellung Berlin GmbH (ed.), Internationale Bauausstellung Berlin 1987, Projektübersicht, Berlin 1987

Behne, Adolf, Der moderne Zweckbau, 2nd ed., Berlin/Frankfurt/Vienna 1964

Bill, Max, 'Report on Brazil, 4' in Architectural Review, London October 1954, pp. 238–39

Boesiger, Willy, Le Corbusier, Oeuvres complètes, Zurich 1970

Das Neue Frankfurt, Frankfurt 1926–30

Davis, Sam, The Architecture of Affordable Housing, Berkeley 1995

Deutscher Werkbund (ed.), Bau und Wohnung, Stuttgart 1927

Doshi, Balkrishna Vithaldas, 'Aranya Township, Indore' in Mimar, Architecture in Development, Singapore, June 1988, pp. 24–29

Doshi, Balkrishna Vithaldas, Contemporary Architects, London 1987

Fathi, Hassan, Gourma, A Tale of Two Villages, Cairo 1969

Frank, Josef, 'Der Volkswohnungspalast' in Der Aufbau, no. 7, Vienna 1926

Frank, Josef, Die internationale Werkbundausstellung in Wien, Vienna 1932

Giedion, Siegfried, Befreites Wohnen, Zurich 1929

Giedion, Siegfrid, Space, Time and Architecture, 3rd. ed., Harvard 1954

Gropius, Walter, 'Report on Brazil, 2', in Architectural Review, London, October 1954, pp. 236–37

Gropius, Walter, Die neue Architektur und das Bauhaus, Frankfurt 1965

Gruen, Victor, The Heart of Our Cities, New York 1964

Hilbersheimer, Ludwig, Entfaltung einer Planungsidee, Berlin/Frankfurt/Vienna 1963

Holl, Steven, Anchoring, New York 1989

Howard, Ebenezer, Tomorrow. A Peaceful Path to Social Reform, London 1898

Iancu, Marcel, 'Arhitecturà socialà' in Contimporanul, IX/93–95, Bucharest 1930, p. 10

Johnston, Lindsay, 'ABBA Housing And Beyond, The Future of Architect-Designed Residential Developments in Australia', in Architectural Design, vol. 73, no. 4, London, July/August 2003

Le Corbusier, 'Vers une Architecture', in L'Esprit Nouveau, 1923 (transl. Towards a New Architecture, London 1931)

Le Corbusier, Entretien avec les étudiants des écoles d'architecture, La Charte d'Athènes, Paris 1957

Käpplinger, Claus, 'Leipzig & Halle. Between New Beginning and Prophecies/Zwischen Aufbruch und Menetekel', in architektur aktuell, Vienna, June 2005

Kidder Smith, G. E., Italy builds. Its Modern Architecture and Native Inheritance, New York 1955

Kulka, Heinrich, Adolf Loos, Vienna 1931

Marcuse, Peter and Ronald van Kempen, Of States and Cities. The Partitioning of Urban Space, Oxford 2002

May, Ernst, 'Hochbau oder Flachbau?' in Der Aufbau, no. 8/9, Vienna 1926

Meier, Richard, Richard Meier, Architect, New York 1984

Migge, Leberecht, Gartenkultur des 20. Jahrhunderts, Jena 1913

Novy, Klaus and Wolfgang Förster, einfach bauen, Vienna 1985

Oud, Jacobus Johannes Pieter, Holländische Architektur, Munich 1929

Roth, Alfred, Die neue Architektur, Zurich 1951

Rudovsky, Bernard, Architecture Without Architects, New York 1964

Schuster, Franz, 'Proletarische Architektur' in Der Aufbau, no. 4, Vienna, 1926, pp. 36–38

Sennett, A. R., Garden Cities In Theory and Practice, London 1905

Sennett, Richard, Flesh And Stone, New York 1994

Sharp, Dennis, Twentieth Century Architecture, A Visual History, New York 1990

Sharp, Thomas, Town Planning, Harmondsworth/New York 1940

Sitte, Camillo, Der Städtebau nach seinen künstlerischen Grundsätzen, Vienna, 1889 (transl. The Art of Building Cities, Westport 1979)

Taut, Bruno, Der neue Wohnbau, Leipzig/Berlin 1927

Techniques et Architecture, nos. 7–8 1948, nos. 5–6, Paris 1951

Viollet-le-Duc, Eugène, Entretien sur l'architecture, Paris 1872

Von Technik und Innendekoration, vol. 36, Stuttgart 1925

Wagner, Otto, Die Großstadt, Vienna 1911

Wettbewerbe, 6–7/2003, Vienna

Zhou, Jinming, Urban Housing Forms, Oxford 2005

Secondary Literature
Sekundärliteratur

Benevolo, Leonardo, *History of Modern Architecture*, London 1971 (transl.: Geschichte der Architektur des 19. und 20. Jahrhunders, Munich 1978)

Benevolo, Leonardo, *The History of the City*, London 1980

Bergmans, Jeroen, 'Havana Good Time' in Wallpaper, London May 2003

Blake, Peter, Le Corbusier, Harmondsworth 1963

Blau, Evelyn, *The Architecture of Red Vienna*, Cambridge/London 1999

Bonfanti, E. et al., *Architettura razionale*, Milan 1975

Broto, Carles, *New Housing Concepts*, Hamburg 2004

Burchard, John and Albert Bush-Brown, *The Architecture of America, a Social and Cultural History*, Boston/Toronto 1966

Chan-Magomedow, Selim O., *Pioniere der sowjetischen Architektur*, Vienna/Berlin 1983

Chemetov, Paul, Marie-Jeanne Dumont and Bernard Marrey, *Paris-Banlieu 1919–1939*, Paris 1989

Cohen, Jean Louis and Monique Eleb, *Casablanca, Colonial Myths and Architectural Ventures*, New York 2002

Collins, George and Christiane Collins, *Camillo Sitte and the Birth of Modern City Planning*, London 1965

Collymore, Peter, *The Architecture of Ralph Erskine*, London 1982

Colqhoun, Ian, *20th-Century British Housing*, Oxford 2004

Dannatt, Trevor, *Modern Architecture in Britain*, London 1959

Derwig, Jan and Erik Mattie, *Functionalism in the Netherlands*, Amsterdam 1995

Dethier, Jean, Thierry Grillet and Alain Guilheux, *La ville, art et architecture en Europe, 1870–1993*, Paris 1994

Devinaz, Danièle, *Promenade à Villeurbanne, Les Gratte-Ciel*, Villeurbanne 2004

Dos Santos, Ana Gabriela, Horia Georgescu and Winfried Nerdinger (eds.), *Modernism in Bucharest*, Salzburg 2001

Dupré, Judith, *Skyscrapers*, New York 1996

Egelius, Mats, *Ralph Erskine, Architect*, Stockholm 1990

Ferlenga, Alberto, *Aldo Rossi*, Milan 1990

Fonatti, Franco, *Giuseppe Terragni*, Vienna 1987

Fontana-Giusti, Gordana and Patrik Schumacher (eds.), *Zaha Hadid, Complete Works*, London 2004

Förster, Wolfgang, *Harry Seidler, Neue Donau Housing Estate Vienna*, Munich 2002

Frampton, Kenneth, *Richard Meier*, Milan 2002

Frampton, Kenneth and Philip Drew, *Harry Seidler*, London 1992

Fundacio Caixa de Pensions (ed.), *Antoni Gaudi*, Barcelona/Vienna 1987

Gallagher, Dominic, *From Here to Modernity* (BBC Open University), London 2005

Gemeentelijke Dienst Volkshuisvesting (ed.), *Sociale Woningbouw Amsterdam*, Amsterdam 1986

Geretsegger, Heinz and Max Peintner, *Otto Wagner 1841–1918*, Salzburg 1964

Ghirardo, Diane, *Mark Mack, A California Architect*, Tübingen/Berlin 1994

Gössel ,Peter and Gabriele Leuthäuser, *Architektur des 20. Jahrhunderts*, Cologne 2001

Goulet, Patrice, *Jean Nouvel*, Paris 1987

Grassi, Giogio, *Das Neue Frankfurt*, Bari 1975

Grinberg, Donald L., *Housing in the Netherlands 1900–1940*, Delft 1982

Hammerbacher, Valerie and Dorothee Keuerleber, *Weißenhofsiedlung*, Stuttgart 2002

Heyer, Paul, *Architects on Architecture. New Directions in America*, New York 1966

Hipp, Hermann, 'Fritz Schumacher's Hamburg' in Lampugnani 1992

Jacobus, John, *Die Architektur unserer Zeit*, Stuttgart 1966

Jetsonen, Sirkkaliisa, *Alvar Aalto's Apartments*, Helsinki 2004

Jodidio, Philip, *Architecture Now!*, Cologne 2001

Joedicke, Jürgen, *A History of Modern Architecture*, London/New York 1959

Johnson, Philip, *Mies van der Rohe*, 2nd ed., New York 1953

Johnson, Philip and Mark Wigley, *Deconstructivist Architecture*, Boston 1988

Kirk, Terry, *The Architecture of Modern Italy*, New York 2005

Kohout, Michal et al. (eds.), *Prague. 20th-century architecture*, Prague 2004

Lampugnani, Vittorio Magnano and Romana Schneider, *Moderne Architektur in Deutschland 1900–1950*, Stuttgart 1992

Lindvall, Jörn (ed.), *The Swedish Art of Building*, Stockholm 1992

Maciuika, John V., *Before the Bauhaus, Architecture, Politics, and the German State, 1890–1920*, New York 2005

Memmott, Paul, 'Aboriginal Housing Has The State of The Art' in *Architecture Australia*, Sydney January/February 2004

Mignot, Claude, *Grammaire des immeubles parisiens*, Paris 2004

Mindlin, Henrique E., *Modern Architecture in Brazil*, London 1956

Moldoveanu, Mihail, *Barcelona. Arquitectura de l'Exuberanca*, Barcelona/Madrid 1996

Münz, Ludwig and Gustav Künstler, *Der Architekt Adolf Loos*, Vienna/Munich 1964

Museum für Gestaltung Zürich (ed.), *Das andere Neue Wohnen*, Zurich 1987

Nerdinger, Winfried, *Tel Aviv, Modern Architecture 1930–1939*, Tübingen/Berlin 1994

Nerdinger, Winfried, Romana Schneider and Wilfried Wang, *Architektur im 20. Jahrhundert, Deutschland*, Munich/London/New York 2000

Noever, Peter (ed.), *Margarete Schütte-Lihotzky. Soziale Architektur, Zeitzeugin eines Jahrhunderts*, Vienna 1993

Norri, Marja-Riitta, Elina Standerskjöld and Wilfried Wang (eds.), *20th-Century Architecture, Finland*, Helsinki/Frankfurt 1999

Novak, Pavel, *Zlinska Architektura 1900–1950*, Zlin 1993

Oosterman, Arjen, *Housing in the Netherlands, Exemplary Architecture in the Nineties*, Rotterdam 1996

Pennink, P. K. A., W. J. Bruyn, 'Het Betondorp' in Forum 19, no. 5/6, Amsterdam 1965

Pevsner, Nikolaus, *Pioneers of Modern Design*, London 1960

Pevsner, Nikolaus, *An Outline of European Architecture*, 6th ed., Harmondsworth 1968

Piessat, Louis, *Tony Garnier*, Lyon 1988

Posener, Julius (ed.), *Ebenezer Howard, Gartenstädte von morgen. Das Buch und seine Geschichte*, Berlin/Frankfurt/Vienna 1968

Pridmore, Jay and George A. Larson, *Chicago Architecture and Design*, New York 2005

Ravetllat Pere, Joan, *Block Housing*, Barcelona 1992

Richards, J.M., *An Introduction to Modern Architecture*, Harmondsworth/New York 1940

Robert, Jean-Paul, 'La Cité Manifeste' in Bauwelt, Berlin, February 2005

Ruegg, Arthur, *Die Doldertalhäuser*, Zurich 1996

Rodriguez, Edoardo Luis, *The Havana Guide. Modern Architecture*, Princeton 2000

Schubert, Dirk, *Hamburger Wohnquartiere*, Berlin 2005

Siegel, Arthur, *Chicago's Famous Buildings*, Chicago/London 1965

Spaeth, David, Mies van der Rohe, London 1985

Tafuri, Manfredo, *Vienna Rossa: La politica residenziale nella Vienna socialista*, Milan 1995

Thau Carsten and Kjelt Vindum, *Arne Jacobsen*, Copenhagen 2002

Wallpaper, London, May 2003

Wegesack, Alexander and Marco Kries (eds.), *Leben unter dem Halbmond. Die Wohnkulturen der arabischen Welt*, Weil am Rhein 2003

Weiss, Srdjan Jovanovic and Sabine von Fischer, 'How to read two Monoliths' in Cabinet Magazine, no. 6, New York 2002

Werkbund, Der österreichische Werkbund, Salzburg 1985

Wilson, Rob, 'Common Ground. Mediating Thresholds Between Public and Private Space in UK Housing Design' in Architectural Design, London, vol. 73, no. 4, July/August 2003, pp. 41–49

Wright, Sylvia Hart, *Sourcebook of Contemporary North American Architecture*, New York 1989

Zevi, Bruno, *Storia dell'Architettura Moderna*, 3rd ed., Turin 1955

INDEX OF PROPER NAMES AND PLACES

PHOTO CREDITS BILDNACHWEIS

Numbers refer to pages. Die Nummern
 beziehen sich auf Seitenzahlen.
 (l=left/links, r=right/rechts, t=top/oben,
 c=center/Mitte, b=bottom/unten)

Aerophoto-Aero Carto – KLM Schiphol
 117 b
Aga Khan Trust for Culture 164,
 165 b, 166
Aga Khan Visual Archive 165 t, c
Agence Gazeau 150, 151 r, 152
Akademie der Künste, Archiv Baukunst,
 Berlin 41
akg-images, Berlin: Paul Almasy 64, 65
Archigram Archives, London 20
Architectuurstudio Herman Hertzberger
 117 l, 123 t
Architekturmuseum der Technischen
 Universität München (ed.), *Modernism
 in Bukarest*, Salzburg 2001 66 l, 67 r
Archiv Burkhard Verlag Ernst Heyer 86
artur, Cologne: Peter Cook/VIEW 76;
 Klaus Frahm 26, 27, 37 l, r;
 Jochen Helle 138, 139 r, 140 t, b;
 Werner Huthmacher 142 t, b
Richard Barnes 124, 125 t
bednorz-photo.de 74, 75 r
Bibliothek der Landesgewerbeanstalt
 in Neurenburg 14
Bildarchiv Hamburg, Christoph Bellin
 30 t, b
Bilderberg, Archiv der Fotografen,
 Hamburg: ITAR-TASS/Alexander
 Saverkin 56
Eve Blau, *The architecture of Red Vienna
 1919–1934*, Cambridge, Mass. 1999
 19 l, 28
Hedrich Blessing 80
Nabil Bonduki, *Affonso Eduardo Reidy*,
 Lisbon 2000 82
Nicolas Borel 153 t, b
Karla Britton, *Auguste Perret*, London/
 New York 2001 70, 71 t, b, 16 l
Martin Charles 123 b
Conway Library, Courtauld Institute
 of Art Gallery, London 47 r
Corbis, Düsseldorf: Royalty-Free 107
Tim Crocker 162 l, 163 t, b

Dannatt 88
Jan Derwig 34, 47 l, 36 l
Richard Dietrich 100
Dolff-Bonekämper 43
Eidgenössische Technische Hochschule
 Zürich (ed.), *Die Doldertalhäuser*,
 Zurich 1996 54 b
Farès el-Dahdah 84 c, b
Hans Engels 49 b
Aarne Ervi, Heikki Havas 91 r
Esto, Mamaroneck: Jeff Goldberg 143 t;
 Ezra Stoller 78, 102, 104 t, 105
João Facó 84 t
Georges Fessy 128, 130
Michael Frank 38 b, 39 b
Katsuaki Furudate 122 t
Gemeentearchief, Amsterdam 13
Heinz Geretsegger, Max Peintner,
 Otto Wagner, Salzburg 1983 12
Ezio Godoli 18 l
Graphische Sammlung Albertina,
 Vienna 17
Gregotti Associati, Milan 122 l
Harvard University/Graduate School
 of Design (ed.), *Ignazio Gardella*,
 Cambridge, Mass. 1986 72 t
Hiroyuki Hirai 149 t, b
Hochschule für angewandte Kunst in Wien
 (ed.), *Der Österreichische Werkbund*,
 Salzburg/Vienna 1985 52 t, b
Eduard Hueber 159 r, l, 147, 148
Timothy Hursley 96, 97, 98, 110 l, 111
Norbert Huse, *Vier Berliner Siedlungen der
 Weimarer Republik*, Berlin 1987 41 b
Institut für Stadtgeschichte, Frankfurt am
 Main 38 t
Irmel Kamp-Bandu, *Tel Aviv Neues Bauen
 1930–1939*, Tübingen 1993 63 l
Anthony King 16 r
Rob Krier Christoph Kohl Architekten
 21, 121 t
Kisho Kurokawa Architect & Associates,
 Tokyo 99 r
Simo Rista, Leppo, Aarne Pietinen 91 l
Jöran Lindvall, *The Swedish Art of
 Building*, Stockholm 1992 32 r
Norman McGrath 108, 109 r
Martin Minces/BsAsFotos 137

Stefan Müller 120 t
Jeroen Musch 141 t
Musée Urbain Tony Garnier,
 painting on wall by Cité de la Création,
 photo: Claude Fezoui 44, 46
NAi Netherlands Architecture Institute,
 Rotterdam 35 t, b, 36 b
Nieuwe Nederlandsche Bouwkunst I,
 1924 15
Nicolas Gail, OeAl 8
Peter Noever (ed.), *Margarete Schütte-
 Lihotzky. Soziale Architektur Zeitzeugin
 eines Jahrhunderts*, Vienna 1993 39 t
Max Plunger 32 l, 33 b, 90 r
Uwe Rau 118, 119 t, 123 t
Pere Joan Ravellat Mira, *Block Housing*,
 Barcelona 1992 127 t, b
Ricardo Bofill/Taller de Arquitectura
 101 t, b
Richard Meier & Partners Architects,
 LLP 103 t, b, 104 b
Jo Reid & John Peck 145 t
Christian Richters 131, 132, 133 t
Simo Rista, Apollo 33 t
Eduardo Luis Rodríguez, *The Havana
 Guide. Modern Architecture 1925–1965*,
 Princeton 2000 85 t, b
Philippe Ruault 145 b, 161
Scala Archives, Florence 55 t, 73 r
Franziska Schmidt 77 t
Franz Schulze, *Mies van der Rohe.
 A Critical Biography*, Chicago/London
 1985 81 l
Eric Sierins of Max Dupain + Associates
 135, 137
Steven Holl Architects 158
Rostislav Švácha, *The Architecture of New
 Prague*, Cambridge, Mass. 1994 53 t, b
Ed Taverne and others, *J.J.P. Oud.
 The Complete Works*, Rotterdam 2001
 19 r, 36 r, 48 b
Carsten Thau, Kjeld Vindum, *Arne Jacob-
 sen*, Copenhagen 2002 60, 61 r, 62
Tigerman McCurry Architects 126 t
Tovatt Architects and Planners, Drottning-
 holm 114, 115, 116
ullstein bild, Berlin: Scheper (Lw) 93
Sybolt Voeten 35

174

Jörn Vogt 51 t, b
Jens Willebrand 117 t
Wissenschaftliches Bildarchiv
    für Architektur, Berlin 40 t, b,
    41 t, 77 b, 92 l
Wohnfonds Wien 28
Nigel Young 144 t
Zaha Hadid Architects 156, 157

© for drawings and plans is held by
    the respective architects

Cover/Umschlag:
MVRDV, 100 WoZoCo'S, Amsterdam
(photographs/Fotos: Christian Richters)
pp. 2–3, 176: de Architekten Cie.,
The Whale, Amsterdam (photograph/
Foto: Keith Collie)
pp. 6–7: Harry Seidler & Associates,
Horizon Apartments, Sydney
(photograph/Foto: Eric Sierins of Max
Dupain + Associates)
p. 25: Lucio Costa, Super Quadra, Brasilia
(photograph/Foto: Julieta Sobral)
pp. 26–27: Anton Brenner, Housing Block
on the Wannsee Railroad Line/Lauben-
ganghaus an der Wannseebahn, Berlin
(photograph/Foto: Hans Engels)
pp. 68–69: Le Corbusier, Unité
d'Habitation, Marseille
(photograph/Foto: Achim Bednorz)
pp. 94–95: Arquitectonica, The Palace,
Miami (photograph/Foto:
Timothy Hursley)
pp. 112–113: Foster & Partners, Albion
Riverside, London
(photograph/Foto: Nigel Young)
p. 155: Santiago Calatrava, Turning Torso,
Malmö (photograph/Foto: Barbara Brug +
Oliver Schuh, www.palladium.de)
p. 171: Dick Greiner, W. Greve, J. B. van
Loghem, Betondorp, Amsterdam
(photograph/Foto: Klaus Frahm/artur)

Prestel Verlag
Königinstrasse 9
80539 Munich
Tel. +49 (0) 89-38 17 09-0
Fax +49 (0) 89-38 17 09-35
www.prestel.de

Prestel Publishing Ltd.
4, Bloomsbury Place
London WC1A 2QA
Tel. +44 (0) 20-73 23-5004
Fax +44 (0) 20-76 36-8004

Prestel Publishing
900 Broadway, Suite 603
New York, NY 10003
Tel. +1 (2 12) 995-2720
Fax +1 (2 12) 995-2733
www.prestel.com

Library of Congress Control Number:
2006900788

The Deutsche Bibliothek holds a record
of this publication in the Deutsche Nation-
albibliografie; detailed bibliographical data
can be found under http://dnb.ddb.de

Prestel books are available worldwide.
Please contact your nearest bookseller or
one of the above addresses for information
concerning your local distributor.

Translation from the German (pp. 8–23):
Paul Aston, San Lorenzo Nuovo

Editorial direction/Projektleitung:
Sandra Leitte
Copyediting/Lektorat:
Christopher Wynne (English),
Sandra Leitte (Deutsch)
Picture research/Bildredaktion:
Sophie Kowall
Design and layout/Gestaltung
und Herstellung: Cilly Klotz
Typesetting/Satz:
Setzerei Max Vornehm, München
Origination/Lithografie: Repro Ludwig,
Zell am See
Printing/Druck: Aumüller, Regensburg
Binding/Bindung: Conzella, Pfarrkirchen

Printed in Germany on acid-free paper
ISBN 3-7913-3529-4
978-3-7913-3529-2

THE AUTHOR DER AUTOR

Wolfgang Förster was born in 1953 in Vienna, Austria, where he studied architecture and political sciences. He has worked for the Vienna Housing Department and is presently Head of the Housing Research Department. He directs a number of international projects in the areas of urban renewal and housing, represents Austria at the UN-ECE Committee for Human Settlements and is chairman of its Social Housing Task Force. He has been working with the Council of Europe and UN-Habitat, lectures at several universities and has numerous publications to his name.

Wolfgang Förster, geboren 1953, studierte Architektur und Politikwissenschaften in Wien. Er arbeitet für die Wohnbauabteilung der Stadt Wien und leitet derzeit deren Wohnbauforschungs- programm. Verantwortlich für eine Reihe internationaler Stadterneuerungs- und Wohnungsbau- projekte, vertritt er Österreich im UN-ECE Committee for Human Settlements und leitet dessen Arbeitsgruppe für Sozialwohnungsbau. Er arbeitet unter anderem in Arbeitsgruppen des Europarats und der UN-Habitat, hält Vorlesungen an mehreren Universitäten und ist Autor zahlreicher Publika- tionen.